Standing Against Anti-Semitism

Understanding the End-Times Significance of this Spiritual Battle

BY HOWARD MORGAN

"Replacing demonic hatred of the Jewish People with Holy Spirit Inspired Love"

Copyright © 2018 by Howard Morgan Ministries

All rights reserved. This book or any portion thereof may not be reproduced or used in any manner whatsoever without the express written permission of the publisher except for the use of brief quotations in a book review or scholarly journal.

First Printing: 2018

ISBN 978-1-329-06498-0

Edited by Deborah Boock, Michael Senger, Susan Gaines and Camille Montgomery.

Cover art created by Michael Senger.

www.howardmorganministries.com

ABOUT THE COVER

Dr. Howard Morgan is holding up the Menorah with a German pastor at the infamous "Selection Point" in the Birkenau Death Camp (also known as Auschwitz II). This was a prophetic act that not only expresses the power of reconciliation between Jews and Gentiles that create the "One New Man" (Ephesians 2:15-16), but also symbolizes how we can work with the God of Israel as He moves toward His eventual victory over the demonic spirits of anti-Semitism, anti-Christ, and Death itself (1 Corinthians 15:26).

ENDORSEMENTS

With his book, "Standing against Anti-Semitism," Howard Morgan has made a significant contribution to the understanding of anti-Semitism that is challenging the world today in many forms, not the least of which is anti-Israelism. In reality, all forms of anti-Semitism, no matter how subtle they may be, are raw manifestations of the morbid, irrational hatred of Jews and all things Jewish that is nothing short of demonic. Dr. Morgan is uniquely gifted to penetrate through the fog of deception and reveal the true nature of the rising tide of anti-Semitism, and he does so with the incisive clarity of spiritual insight.

John D. Garr, Ph.D.
President
Hebraic Heritage Christian College

It is very likely that the last great apostasy of the Church will be how she stands with Israel and the Jewish people. If we do not grasp God's covenant and heart for His host people, we will be deceived and on the wrong side of history. Howard's book is an excellent tool to help the Church understand this and to repent for centuries of anti-Semitism and replacement theology, a theology that assumes God is finished with Israel and that the Church has replaced her.

Don Finto
Pastor Emeritus Belmont Church Nashville, TN
Founder & Director of the Caleb Company
Author of God's Promise and the Future of Israel, Your People Shall Be My People, and, Prepare! For the End Time Harvest

DEDICATION

This book is dedicated to those authentic disciples of the Kingdom of God who desire to participate in God's plan for the restoration of the Body of Christ to her Biblical relationship and responsibility to the Jewish people. May it prove to be a valuable weapon in your battle against the twin demonic principalities of anti-Semitism and anti-Christ. May God give you great victories as His *"servants who find pleasure in Zion's stones, and feel pity for her dust"* and may you fulfill your destiny in God's end-time plan to *"Build up Zion and then appear in His Glory*! (Psalm 102:14,16).

ACKNOWLEDGEMENTS

Thanks to my beloved wife Janet for everything she has always done. To Dr. Jennifer Scrivner, a true lover of Zion, for her input into the very first draft. To Dr. John Garr, for his excellent editorial advice and most valuable friendship. To Camille Montgomery for her eye for details and perceptive questions. To Susan Gaines, my professional editor and good friend, who did what all good editors and friends do. May all your labors bear much fruit for the Kingdom of God!

TABLE OF CONTENTS

ABOUT THE COVER i
ENDORSEMENTS ii
DEDICATION iii
ACKNOWLEDGEMENTS iv
INTRODUCTION AND OVERVIEW 1

    Restoration #1: Understanding that Christians are "Grafted into" Israel and Have "Jewish Roots." 4

    Restoration #2: Understanding the Biblical Relationship and Responsibility of the Church to the Jewish People. 5

    Restoration #3: Standing with Israel for the Fulfillment of the Purposes of God 5

CHAPTER 1 – A SEASON OF RESTORATION 7

    Our "Jewish or Hebraic Roots" 7

    A Time of Restoration 13

    The Church's Biblical Relationship and Responsibility to the Jewish people. 15

    Testifying to the Jewish People 17

    A Prophetic Vision 22

    God's Love for the Nations 23

CHAPTER 2 – AN APPOINTED TIME FOR HEALING LOVE, WHY NOW? 27

    Psalm 102:13-18 28

CHAPTER 3 – SATAN'S MASTER PLAN TO PREVENT THE RETURN OF JESUS 37

    Strategy #1: 40

        A) Kill all the Jews 40

        B) Assimilate the Jews 41

    Strategy #2: 45

  Use the Church as an instrument of death and assimilation.....45

 A Connection Many Christians Fail to See..................46

 Anti-Semitism is Supernatural and can be Subtle................50

CHAPTER 4 – FIGHTING THIS SPIRITUAL BATTLE..............55

 A Prophetic Picture of this Warfare..........................57

CHAPTER 5 – UNDERSTANDING YOUR....................61
RELATIONSHIP TO HISTORY.................................61

 If all of this is true, what can we do about it?...............65

 What if…?...72

CHAPTER 6 – DOCTRINES OF DEMONS........................73
VS. BIBLICAL TRUTHS.....................................73

 Lie # 1 - The Jewish people "killed Christ" and therefore all Jews of every generation are guilty of the crime of deicide (killing God)...73

 Lie # 2 - God rejected and abandoned the Jewish people as their punishment for the crime of killing Jesus..........................75

 Lie # 3 - The Church replaced the rejected Jews and became the "new" or "spiritual" Israel...................................75

 Lie # 4 – The Church must persecute the Jewish people as a punishment for their crime of deicide...........................76

 Lie # 5 - This "punishment" of the Jews serves as a warning to all people who reject Christ......................................77

 Doctrines of Demons......................................77

CHAPTER 7 – SHARING YOUR FAITH WITH THE JEWISH PEOPLE...81

 The Importance and Power of Unconditional Love and Evangelism...81

 Beware of Hidden Agendas 84

CHAPTER 8 – HOW DO I GET STARTED?......................91

 Practical Guidelines and Suggestions 91

CONTACT INFORMATION.....................................97

Standing Against Anti-Semitism

Understanding the End-Times Significance of this Spiritual Battle

"Replacing demonic hatred of the Jewish People with Holy Spirit Inspired Love"

INTRODUCTION AND OVERVIEW

Anti-Semitism is more than merely a human, social, economic, religious or political phenomenon. It is a major satanic strategy focused on the persecution or destruction of the Jewish people. The real goal of anti-Semitism is to hinder or even prevent the second coming of Jesus (Yeshua) the Messiah. Seen in this way, we can recognize that anti-Semitism is actually the spirit of anti-Christ in disguise. Once we recognize that these two major demonic principalities work in tandem for the same purpose, we can see how they have worked together historically and continue to do so today.

It is crucial to understand that *the Jewish people are Satan's target, not because they are Jews, but because they hold a pivotal place in God's plan to return Messiah to the earth* (Zechariah 12:10-11, 14:4; Matthew 23:39; Acts 3:21; Romans 11:15).

To understand the spiritual nature of anti-Semitism, we must understand two things the Scriptures teach. First, God's plans and purposes for the Jewish people. Second, the significance of the relationship and responsibility the authentic Body of Christ has with the Jewish people for the fulfillment of those plans and purposes.

As we study the Scriptures and history, we see that Satan has used multileveled strategies in his attempts to thwart those plans and purposes. Church and Jewish history show us how he used various *"doctrines of demons"* and *"activities of evil spirits"* (1 Timothy 4:1) to accomplish several secondary objectives. When these are joined, we see how they are focused on the attainment of his primary goal, hindering or preventing the return of the Messiah to establish the Kingdom of God on the earth.

Some of those goals focused on uprooting the authentic Body of Christ from her "Jewish or Hebraic Roots" and replacing those "Roots" with Greek, Roman and Pagan beliefs and practices. Having been uprooted, the "Church" became aberrant, and a new non-Biblical religion emerged that is known historically as "Christianity." Rejecting her "Biblical Roots" and relationship with the Jewish people, the

Church adopted several demonically inspired theological beliefs that created an antagonistic, hostile attitude toward the Jews. These beliefs were also used to justify their horrific persecution of the Jewish people.

Satan was able to take the truths of the New Covenant Scriptures – a book fundamentally teaching people to live lives of faith and love – and either replace its core teachings altogether with demonic lies posing as Church doctrines, or so distort them that the ignorant masses – who by and large were illiterate – could be manipulated into persecuting the Jewish people believing it was the "will of God." These lies enabled Satan to banish the New Covenant Scriptures from the Jewish people. How could they even touch a book that they believed was "Christianity's Instruction Manual" for their pain and suffering.

These satanic strategies produced two major negative outcomes. The Church, in direct disobedience to the clear command of God to *"not be arrogant toward the Jewish people"* (Romans 11:18), was *"cut off"* from the life-giving *"Roots"* of Israel's *"Olive Tree"* (Romans 11:22). This arrogant rebellion opened the door to all the other demonic aberrancies that influenced the Church, and it descended into centuries of spiritual darkness. The Church was no longer authentic because it was no longer apostolic, prophetic or evangelistic. The religion of "Christianity" neither made nor matured disciples for the Kingdom of God, but rather merely created members of that religion. Thank God that throughout history, and continuing to this day, there has always been a "remnant" – those individuals and communities of faith that are authentic expressions of the Body of Christ.

This aberrant Church developed horrific anti-Semitic theologies. They ranged from one extreme that the Jews should be violently persecuted and even killed, to another, that the Jews are a discarded and irrelevant people and should be rejected and avoided. Another aberrant theology told Jews who came to faith in Jesus that they could no longer remain Jews. They had to renounce and reject anything and everything that connected them with their Jewish identity, culture, traditions, religion or people. They had to replace their "Jewishness" with whatever their "Christian" leaders demanded of them. The goal of this "doctrine of demons" is utter and complete assimilation that annihilates any form of Jewish identity.

Another erroneous theology actively proclaimed by some leaders today, is that the Jewish people should not be evangelized because they have their own Covenant with God and don't need Jesus. Of course, if this was true, why would Jesus say that He came for the *"Lost sheep of the House of Israel"* (Matthew 15:24)? Why would the Jewish Apostle Peter proclaim that God sent Jesus to the Jewish people first (Acts 3:26)? Why would another Jewish Apostle, Paul, declare, *"I am not ashamed of the Gospel, for it is the power of God for salvation to everyone who believes, to the Jew first and also to the Gentiles"* (Romans 1:16)? Why would Paul always go to Synagogues to preach that Jesus was the Messiah to the Jewish people if the Jews did not also need to believe? Of course, both Jewish people and Gentiles need Jesus!!

The Spirit of anti-Semitism is focused on eliminating Jews as a "distinct" people and Israel as a "distinct" nation. This is in direct opposition to the revealed purposes of God which declare the calling and immutability of the Jewish people (Deuteronomy 7:6, 14:2; Leviticus 20:26; Jeremiah 31:36-37). If the Jewish people were destroyed via genocide or total assimilation, there would be no Jews or people who identify themselves as Jews on the earth. Then the covenant promises of God concerning the Jewish people could never be fulfilled. If the Word of God fails to be fulfilled, Jesus would not be able to return, and Satan could remain the *"god of this world"* (2 Corinthians 4:4; John 14:30; 16:11; 1 John 5:19) forever.

This is Satan's goal. But, as the Scriptures themselves declare, *"the Word of God cannot be broken"* (John 10:35). Jesus Himself declared: *"For truly I say to you, until heaven and earth pass away, not the smallest letter or stroke shall pass from the Torah until all is accomplished"* (Matthew 5:18; Luke 16:17). The coming of the Lord is *"as certain as the dawn"* (Hosea 6:3).

Additionally, "Christianized" anti-Semitic theologies, doctrines, and beliefs have another demonically inspired theme in common. That is to hide the truth of the Gospel of Salvation from the Jewish people and treat them with disdain, contempt, and hatred. In this way, anything to do with Jesus is forbidden and rejected by the Jews, and the Church rejects anything to do with the Jews. This has been and continues to be a major part of Satan's master plan.

We must understand these things in order to recognize and effectively expose the sources of anti-Semitism, and as God gives us the abilities, stand against its activities and eradicate its effects.

Christians who resist anti-Semitism and stand with the Jewish people play a significant role in this spiritual battle. Every disciple of Jesus the Jewish Messiah must understand that the Body of Christ has "Hebraic Roots" and a Biblical relationship and responsibility to the Jewish people. We are living in a day when God is moving by His Holy Spirit to restore this understanding to the Church. He is challenging His people to take their place in the ultimate spiritual conflict that "Prepares the Way" for the Return of the Lord (Isaiah 40:3; Matthew 3:3; Mark 1:3; Luke 3:4).

This restoration has three specific dynamics.

Restoration #1: Understanding that Christians are "Grafted into" Israel and Have "Jewish Roots."

All Christians must understand that Romans 11 teaches us that we have a *"grafted-in"* relationship among the *"natural branches"* of Israel's *"Olive Tree."* From this supernatural connection, we can receive the spiritual life provided by the *"Anointed Roots"* of this Tree (Romans 11:17). This anointing imparts an understanding and empowerment that enables each believer to be delivered from centuries of Greek, Roman, and Pagan aberrant influences upon the "Christian" religion and grow to fruitful spiritual maturity (Ephesians 4:13; Colossians 1:28). Recognizing this supernatural relationship, we can be restored to God's original intention for the Church and the Jewish people. This brings us to:

Restoration #2: Understanding the Biblical Relationship and Responsibility of the Church to the Jewish People.

As we understand that we have this *"grafted in"* relationship with the natural branches of the *"Olive Tree"* and share in its *"Roots,"* we also learn that we have a responsibility to lovingly witness to the Jewish people about how their Messiah changed our lives. All believers are called to *"show mercy"* through acts of loving-kindness to the Jewish people, as we have *"received mercy"* from the God of Israel. Additionally, we are called to provoke them to *"spiritual jealousy."* One way this can happen is through supernatural demonstrations of the reality of the Kingdom of God (Romans 11:11, 31, 15:19; 1 Corinthians 2:4-5, 4:20; 1 Thessalonians 1:5).

Restoration #3: Standing with Israel for the Fulfillment of the Purposes of God

The Church must stand alongside the Jewish people and the nation of Israel. This does not mean we have to agree with or support everything the Jewish people, or the Israelis, or their government, says or does. However, we must intercede for them that God's prophetic purposes come to pass (Psalm 122:6; Genesis 12:3). We must also exercise our spiritual authority over their demonic adversaries that seek to prevent those purposes from being fulfilled. (Luke 10:19; Matthew 28:18-19; Ephesians 1:20-23, 3:10). We must also testify to Israel's human enemies about the purposes of God for the Jewish people and for the land of Israel that are revealed in the pages of Holy Scripture. This testimony must also include a clear proclamation of the Gospel, accompanied by similar acts of loving-kindness and supernatural demonstrations of the power of the God of Israel, so that all people everywhere will have the opportunity to come to faith in Jesus.

CHAPTER 1 – A SEASON OF RESTORATION

The Holy Spirit is restoring to the Church an understanding of the prophetic significance of her Biblical "Jewish or Hebraic Roots." This is in conjunction with His work of delivering the Body of Christ from the aberrancies of historic Christianity and restoring, among other things, authentic apostolic and prophetic ministries that are foundational for the healthy proper functioning of the Body of Christ (Ephesians 2:20-22). The confluence of these restorations will equip the Body of Christ for end time ministry so that it can be brought to unity and maturity (Ephesians 4:13). God is raising up ministries around the world that are teaching the Church about these restorations and their prophetic implications and significance.

As the Lord restores the Church to her "Jewish/Hebraic Roots," He will also restore her Biblical relationship and responsibility to the Jewish people. We are called to love, pray for and testify to the Jewish people about the Messiahship of Jesus. Additionally, because God loves the world and is not willing that any should perish (2 Peter 3:9), we are also called to love, pray for, and testify to all nations (especially those hostile to the Jews) about God's purposes for them, for the Jewish people and the land of Israel.

Our "Jewish or Hebraic Roots"

The "Jewish/Hebraic Roots" of the Christian faith are an extremely serious issue for the Body of Christ. The understanding of, and participation with, these "Roots," has profound prophetic implications and ramifications. The historic rejection of these "Roots" has had an extremely negative impact on the life, ministry, and fruitfulness of the Church. In Romans 11, the apostle Paul warned every Christian against becoming arrogant toward the Jewish people. In very clear and strong terms, he proclaimed that the Church would be cut off from the very life of God if it became arrogant in its attitude toward the Jewish people and rejected them. He said:

"But if some of the branches were broken off, and you,

being a wild olive, were grafted in among them and became partaker with them of the rich root of the Olive Tree, **do not be arrogant toward the branches**; *but if you are arrogant, remember that it is not you who supports the root, but the root supports you. You will say then, "Branches were broken off so that I might be grafted in." Quite right, they were broken off for their unbelief, but you stand by your faith.* **Do not be arrogant, but fear**; *for if God did not spare the natural branches, He will not spare you, either. Behold then the kindness and severity of God; to those who fell, severity, but to you, God's kindness, if you continue in His kindness; otherwise you also will be cut off"* (Romans 11:17-22).

The Church disobeyed this apostolic command, rejected her "Jewish Roots," and became arrogant toward the Jewish people. Because of that, the Church was cut off from the life of God and was infected by the beliefs and practices inherent in the pagan Greco-Roman world. Having been removed from her Biblical "Roots" in Israel's "Olive Tree," three powerful forces combined - the humanistic philosophies of the Greeks, the governmental structures of the Romans, and their Pagan religious and superstitious beliefs – to create a new **non-Biblical religion** that became known as "Christianity."

Instead of being the Biblically based supernatural faith community that had organic relationships focused on mutual spiritual nourishment for the purpose of bringing every member to maturity in Christ (Colossians 1:28-29; Ephesians 4:11-16), the Church became a hierarchical monarchy which focused on maintaining its own institutional power by claiming Biblical authority while disobeying its teachings. It created among other things, non-Biblical clergy-laity distinctions, the establishment of an unscriptural priesthood with its power to administer "sacraments" (rituals that impart salvation), and many other non-Biblical doctrines and dogmas. Seeking to maintain control, it did not create a literate people. Under the guise of not wanting to allow confusion or "misinterpretation," it also forbade the so-called "laity" from reading the Scriptures (if they could read at all). To further ad-

CHAPTER 1 – A SEASON OF RESTORATION

vance its control, this aberrant Church sought to prevent the Scriptures from being translated into the language of the people. Many were martyred for the "crime" of translating the Scriptures.

Satan did not then, nor does he now, want people to read the Bible for themselves. He constantly fights to undermine its authority and present-day applicability. Without an educated Biblically literate people, the Church is easily influenced or even controlled by Satan himself. God commanded Israel to be a literate people. He commanded them to *"write the commandments on their doorposts and gates"* and *"teach them to their children"* (Deuteronomy 6:7-9, 11:19-20). One must be able to read and write to do this. Without a personal knowledge of the Bible, one cannot grow as a true disciple. Aberrant churches do not make, nor mature, true disciples. They make religious "churchgoers."

The Church established non-Jewish theologies that rejected the Torah (which neither Jesus nor Paul did – Matthew 5:17; Romans 3:3; 2 Timothy 3:16). It replaced the Feasts of the Lord (Leviticus 23), with all of their prophetic meaning and spiritual instructions, with their own pagan-based "holy days." For example, the Nicene Council in 325 AD declared that the Church should celebrate Jesus' resurrection at "Easter" (the name itself has pagan roots). "Easter" is to be held on the first Sunday following the full moon after the Spring equinox, instead of at Passover, according to the Jewish calendar, when it actually happened.

This aberrant Church eventually transformed Jesus the Jewish Messiah, the King of the Jews, into a kind of "Cosmic Christ" who has no recognizable human ethnic identity. This was not limited to the Roman Catholic Church. Although it rejected many of the errors of Catholicism, much of Protestantism also rejected its "Jewish Roots" and was similarly infected.

We have met many Christians, who express surprise and even shock when we teach about the Jewishness of Jesus. We have had people tell us that Jesus was a Baptist because he was baptized by John the "Baptist," or that he was a Catholic because certainly his mother Mary was a Catholic!

Not recognizing the importance of understanding the Jewishness of Jesus and the "Hebraic Roots" of the New Covenant opens up many doors for deception. Beginning to understand these truths and their manifold ramifications closes those doors to deception and opens many new ones for deepening our walk with the Lord.

Another tragic consequence of the Church's rejection of her "Jewish Roots" was the adoption of the practice of persecuting those of differing theologies and practices. Instead of embracing the Biblical truth of diversity as a God-given vehicle for spiritual growth and maturity in Christ (1 Corinthians 12:12-27), where everyone is free to accept or reject various beliefs and practices (Romans 14; 1 Thessalonians 5:19-20) - "uniformity" i.e. conformity to external forms, (as opposed to authentic heart to heart *"unity of the Spirit"* (Ephesians 4:3, 13)) - was enforced at the point of a sword.

I personally believe that a demonic "spirit of murder" – remember Jesus taught us that Satan *"was a murderer from the beginning"* (John 8:44) – entered into the heart of the Church when she believed the demonic lie that blamed the Jews for the death of Jesus and accused them as "Christ killers." The life-giving truth of the Messiah's death as a voluntary atonement for humanity's sins (John 10:17-18), was twisted and perverted into a demonic doctrine that opened the door for massive satanically inspired mayhem and murder.

Instead of proclaiming the life-changing truth of the atoning sacrifice of the Messiah (Isaiah 53; John 4:10; 1 Corinthians 15:3), and the power of His resurrection (Romans 1:14; Philippians 3:10), the Church accused all Jewish people everywhere for all time of killing Him. The "Church" wielded this satanic lie of "Deicide" as a sword that brought suffering and death, instead of God's message of salvation and eternal life to generations of Jewish people. Satan used this lie to bring dishonor and reproach upon the Name of Jesus, rather than what the truth is intended to bring, Glory and Honor to His Name!

Operating under the demonic delusion that the "Jews killed Christ," the Church was further deceived into believing that she was called to punish the Jews for their "crime" and set about executing God's "vengeance" upon the Jewish people. Rivers of blood were shed as

CHAPTER 1 – A SEASON OF RESTORATION

this misguided false "Church" not only rejected her "Jewish Roots" but inflamed hatred for the Jewish people. Using their demonic theologies as a justification, "Christian" mobs were incited to murderous frenzied mayhem, believing that it was their "Christian responsibility" to kill Jews. Persecution and death became a viable, sanctified and "holy" means for dealing with God's "enemies." Of course, this was in complete opposition to the commands of Jesus to *"love your enemies"* (Matthew 5:44; Luke 6:27).

History has recorded many true disciples of the Kingdom who saw this and many other unscriptural and evil practices, and stood against them. They were branded as "apostates and heretics" and were persecuted, tortured and martyred for the truths of the Bible. They were sacrificed on the altar of Biblical truth and faith by this demonic "spirit of murder." Such people will gloriously wear a *"martyr's crown"* (Revelation 2:8-11).

The Church was so aberrant and deceived that it carried out the commands of the "spirit of murder" while believing it was the "true Church" obeying its "Lord." This demonized Church, while killing her victims, would often shout praise to her "god." But, her god was not the God of the Bible, but the evil, devious malevolent usurper, the devil himself. The tragic irony of Church history is that instead of being a redeemed community carrying the "good news" of God's revelation of love, salvation, and eternal life, it became a demonized and deceived instrument of hatred, suffering, and death for generations of Jewish people.

Additionally, the Church's rejection of her "Jewish Roots" and the Jewish people caused her aberrancies to increase with devastating effect. Its "members" were robbed of any Biblically based spiritual life. Biblical truth was hidden and the message of the Gospel was so distorted that Gentiles in the Church (they should not be called real "Christians") were not privileged to hear the true Gospel of Salvation and redemptive love. They simply became part of a religious institution. No one was *"born from above"* (John 3:3-8), or *"baptized in the Holy Spirit"* (Matthew 3:11; Luke 3:16; John 1:33; Acts 1:5, 2:4, 11:16). There was no discipleship to spiritual maturity (Colossians 1:28-29), or demonstrations and manifestations of the Fruits and Gifts of the Holy Spirit (1 Corinthians 12:1-11, 14:1-33; Galatians 5:22-23), and there was no world evangelism (Matthew 28:19; Luke 24:47).

Satan succeeded in robbing the Church of her spiritual life (John 10:10) and created a massive spiritual vacuum that allowed his lies to fuel his evil murderous plans.

Instead of enjoying a life full of the benefits of salvation that could have brought glory and honor to the Name of Jesus, these benighted people were manipulated to bring dishonor and reproach upon His name. The people did this believing they were "obeying God" because they did what the Church leaders instructed them to do.

Instead of being filled with the "Light and Love" that motivated Jesus to *"weep over Jerusalem"* (Luke 19:41), and the Apostle Paul to *"carry great sorrow and unceasing grief in* his *heart,"* even *"wishing himself accursed"* if it meant the salvation of his people (Romans 9:1-3), the Church became "Dark and Demonic." It was this demonic darkness that inspired the Church to perpetrate its many crimes.

How great will the Judgment of God be upon those leaders! How different the history of the world, and particularly the Jewish people would have been, if the Church leaders had taught love and not hate!

The horrific practice of persecuting those who disagreed with and dared to oppose the authority of the "religious powers that be," affirmed to the Jewish people that their assessment of "Christianity" (both Catholic and Protestant versions) – and the "Jesus Christ" it proclaimed to represent – was fraudulent. The fact that "Christian" theology concerning the Jews was abhorrent and their treatment of the Jews vicious, only served to harden the hearts of the Jews toward Jesus. This treatment would harden the heart of anyone who was victimized by such a "religion."

Do not think that the "spirit of murder" has ceased its activities in the "Church" because we live in a more "civilized" era. It has simply changed its strategies and tactics. Instead of physically killing its enemies, it seeks other ways to "murder" them. How many lives, families, churches, and ministries have been destroyed by wicked words of gossip, backbiting, and slander? It is this spirit that motivates Church leaders and members to "shoot their own wounded" with judgmental fault-finding, constant criticism, damning accusations and painful rejection.

Why don't more local pastors frequently meet to encourage and support one another? Why do many pastors secretly rejoice when another pastor falls or when other churches do not thrive? Why are others envious instead of rejoicing at another's success? Where is the unity that Jesus Himself prayed for (John 17:20-23) and the Apostle Paul urged us to in Ephesians 4:3 and 13?

All of this is evidence that the "spirit of murder" is still influencing the Church in many ways and in many places. This demonic principality must be exposed, confronted, renounced, and rejected. It must be replaced with LOVE. As 1 Corinthians 13 teaches us, LOVE should be the first and foremost characteristic of the authentic Body of Christ and the fruit that most clearly defines her reputation.

For all these centuries that the Lord Jesus has remained in Heaven, the "Great Intercessor" (Romans 8:34; Hebrews 7:25), has been praying for his Bride to become that glorious expression of His nature, which is essentially LOVE, for GOD IS LOVE! (1 John 4:8, 16).

A Time of Restoration

Thank God, we are living in a day of restoration. Believers from every corner of the earth are receiving genuine Holy Spirit inspired revelation concerning the "Jewish Roots" of their faith. Please understand that when I am talking about "Jewish Roots," I am not talking about modern day Rabbinic or traditional Judaism. This religion was created by Rabbis as a result of the destruction of the Temple in 70 AD and the following exile of the Jews from the land of Israel. While we can gain much spiritual insight from various Jewish sources, Rabbinic Judaism is not the model for the Body of Christ. We are called to follow the principles and patterns laid out for us in both the Hebrew Scriptures and the New Testament. As this restoration continues to unfold and we understand more of those principles and patterns, the Body of Christ is being set free from the aberrancies of the "Christian religion" and is seeking God for more Biblically authentic ways of sharing life together and cooperating for more fruitful ministry.

Part of this restoration includes learning to read the Scriptures from a Hebraic perspective. As we do this, we also learn to think Hebraically. What this means, essentially, is that we put our focus on our supernatural relationship with God by faith, rather than depending solely upon our reason and intellect. Human reasoning and intellectual understanding are the central features of the Greek philosophical foundations of all Western humanistic belief systems (2 Corinthians 4:18; Proverbs 3:5-6). **All ideologies built on this foundation have the same result; man is exalted, and God is either ignored, minimized, or rejected altogether.**

As our understanding of these "Roots" increases, we will see more clearly the relationship between the Body of Christ and the Jewish people in the fulfillment of God's present prophetic purposes. This creates a desire for the Body of Christ to be all that the Lord Jesus intends for His Bride. We can no longer settle for just man-made religion. We desire intimacy with God and a life of fruitfulness that gives Him pleasure (2 Corinthians 5:9; Ephesians 5:10). This is part of what is imparted to us by being connected to our "Jewish Roots."

During one particularly powerful time of corporate worship the Lord showed me that the "anointing" in the "Roots" of Israel's "Olive Tree" (Romans 11:17) acts as an "anti-venom," or an antidote to the "venom" of the "Spirit of Religion" and anti-Semitism the devil uses to infect the Body of Christ. As we receive this antidote, this "anti-venom," we are set free to understand the differences between the "religion of Christianity" and the authentic Body of Christ. We learn the difference between man-made religion, with its many non-Biblical aberrancies, and that which is the authentic apostolic, prophetic *"faith which was once for all delivered to the saints"* (Jude 1:3).

CHAPTER 1 – A SEASON OF RESTORATION

The dual foundational gift ministries of apostles and prophets are being restored to the Body of Christ to bring it to maturity and the fulfillment of its destiny in the world (Ephesians 2:20, 4:11-15). A mature Church will be able, by the wisdom and power of the Holy Spirit, to face and resolve the serious issues that keep her divided, loveless, spiritually immature and generally powerless. This is a *"glorious Church without spot or blemish"* (Ephesians 5:27), without the fleshly insecurities, pride, self-centeredness, divisions, and territorialism that divide her and greatly limit her effectiveness. This is a Church that is mature, unified and full of Glory, Power, and Love. This is the Bride ready for the return of Her Groom. These are the kind of people that can provoke natural Israel to spiritual jealousy! (Romans 11:11, 14). Amen!!

The Church's Biblical Relationship and Responsibility to the Jewish people.

When the Church rejected her "Jewish Roots," she not only became infected with Greek, Roman, and Pagan influences, she also rejected her Biblical relationship and responsibility to the Jewish people. Falling into centuries of spiritual darkness, the Church developed an ongoing adversarial relationship with the Jews. The demonic infection of anti-Semitism spread through the Church as a malignant cancer that affected the entire history of the Christian religion.

One of the most powerful perpetrators of this evil was the great preacher John Chrysostom (which means "golden tongue"). Chrysostom was a revered bishop of the 4th century, known for his many inspiring sermons and lovely devotional writings extolling his love for Jesus. But he was also responsible for preaching eight horrific sermons in which he dreadfully vilified and demonized all the Jewish people, declaring in these messages entitled *Homilies Against the Jews,* **"It is the duty of all Christians to hate the Jews."**

In the 16th century, Martin Luther was the preeminent leader of the Protestant Reformation and restorer of the doctrine of "salvation by faith." He was also the restorer of the Bible as the ultimate authority for the "priesthood of all believers," not the Roman Catholic Church.

In his last years, he was greatly infected by these same spirits. Denouncing the Jewish people in the most horrific ways, his writings became the spiritual soil that eventually helped to birth the Holocaust. There is much blood on his hands.

Luther wrote in his book *On the Jews and their Lies* (1543):

> **"What shall we Christians do with this rejected and condemned people, the Jews? They are venomous, bitter worms and disgusting vermin, they are all thieves and should be deported to Palestine...I shall give you my sincere advice.**
>
> **First: Set fire to their Synagogues or schools and bury and cover with dirt whatever will not burn, so that no man will ever again see a stone or cinder of them.**
>
> **Second: I advise that their houses also be razed and destroyed.**
>
> **Third: I advise that all their prayer books and Talmudic writings, in which idolatry, lies, cursing, and blasphemy are taught be taken from them.**
>
> **Fourth: I advise that their rabbis be forbidden to teach henceforth on pain of the loss of life and limb.**
>
> **Fifth: I advise that safe-conduct on the highways be abolished for the Jews, let them stay at home.**
>
> **Sixth: I advise that usury be prohibited to them and that all cash and treasure of silver and gold be taken from them and put aside for safekeeping.**
>
> **Seventh: I recommend putting a flail, an ax, a hoe, a spade, a distaff or a spindle into the hands of young, strong Jews and Jewesses and letting them earn their bread by the sweat of their brow."**

CHAPTER 1 – A SEASON OF RESTORATION

That such highly influential leaders, who proclaimed much love for the Lord, who knew the Biblical commandments to *"love your neighbor"* (Luke 10:27) and *"love your enemies"* (Matthew 5:44) could spew out such vile, venomous hatred for the Jewish people is graphic testimony to the enormous deceiving power of the demonic principality known as "Anti-Semitism."

Across the spectrum of Christian history, many so-called "leaders" were influenced by this spirit. Motivated by ungodly desires, including deeply rooted spiritual and psychological insecurities, financial greed, racial prejudice and the desire for power, they manipulated the masses and inspired them to perpetrate dreadful, hate-filled crimes upon the Jewish people.

Instead of obeying the commandment of Romans 11:31 to *"show mercy"* to the Jewish people and of Romans 11:11, to *"provoke them to jealousy"* and faith in Jesus, the Church's hatred and persecution of the Jews instead provoked them to deeply rooted bitterness, profound resentment, great anger and further entrenched rejection of Jesus as their Messiah.

Testifying to the Jewish People

What will cause the Jewish people, who are deeply rooted in their national, cultural, intellectual, historical and religious rejection of Jesus to receive Him as their Messiah? I believe that the answer to that question begins with the fact that there is a sovereign move of the Holy Spirit stirring hearts of believers around the world to recognize their Biblical relationship and responsibility to the Jewish people. As this restoration continues to unfold, there will be many opportunities for the Body of Christ to testify to the Jewish people about their Messiah.

History records many individual believers who, operating in the love and power of the Holy Spirit, provoked individual Jews to spiritual jealousy and then to faith in their Messiah. What happens on an individual level can happen on a corporate level. Just as spiritually mature individual believers have been able to provoke individual Jews to spiritual jealousy, is it not possible that spiritually mature believers from all the nations would be able to provoke all the Jewish people to spiritual jealousy and faith in their Messiah? Is this not the heart of God expressed by the great Jewish apostle Paul in Romans 11? It is exactly because of this that the enemy so vigorously fights all efforts to mature the Body of Christ and does all he can to keep it from its Biblical relationship and responsibility to the Jewish people.

I believe that this current move of reconciliation and testimony is a preparation for the fulfillment of Zechariah 12:10. This prophecy speaks of an overwhelming outpouring of the Holy Spirit that reveals to the Jewish people that Jesus is the one they "pierced" and that He is indeed their longed-for Messiah. That event will not come "out of the blue" without any warning, preparation, or context. I do not believe that the entire Jewish world will just wake up one morning and be overwhelmed with the presence of the Holy Spirit and have the age-ending dramatic encounter that reveals to them that Jesus is their Messiah. That is not the way God has manifested Himself to the nation of Israel in their Scriptural history, nor is it the way He has manifested Himself during times of authentic revivals in the history of the Church. The outpouring of the Spirit is always within the context of intercessory prayer, preaching (the proclamation of truth), and teaching (the explanation of those truths). Of course, many individuals have had life-changing encounters with God without such a context, but God then used these unique individuals to pray for, instruct and lead the others.

Before there is ever an outpouring of the Spirit of God in revival or an outpouring of the wrath of God in judgment, there are always preparatory prophetic proclamations. Amos 3:7 teaches us that *"Surely the Lord God does nothing unless He reveals His secret counsel to His servants the prophets."* It is these anointed servants who then declare what the Lord is going to do. For example, before the flood, God sent Noah to preach a message of repentance (2 Peter 2:5), even while building the ark, which was in itself a prophetic warning of the coming judgment. In response to the prayers of the Jewish people (Exodus 3:7, 9), God sent Moses with a warning to Pharaoh before the history-changing demonstrations of His power, which led to Israel's exodus from Egypt.

CHAPTER 1 – A SEASON OF RESTORATION

Before the living God manifested Himself to Israel at Mount Sinai, Moses gave them preparatory warnings and instructions (Exodus 19:10-11). Before the destruction of the first Temple and the Babylonian captivity, God's prophets repeatedly issued strong warnings. Daniel 9:24-26 declared the time of the Messiah's first coming, and John the Baptist prepared the way for the ministry of Jesus by preaching a message of repentance (Matthew 3:3). Jesus' atoning death and resurrection prepared the way for the arrival of the Holy Spirit (John 7:38-39). He instructed the disciples to wait for the outpouring of the Holy Spirit who would empower them to be His witnesses (Acts 1:4). All revivals in history, accompanied by mighty demonstrations of the presence and power of the Holy Spirit, were preceded by clear prophetic proclamations, explanations, and deep, fervent intercession.

God's plan is to use the intercession and testimony of Gentile believers from the nations of the world to arouse the Jewish people to the truth and reality of the Messiahship of Jesus. **The authentic Body of Christ – people filled with the love and power of the Holy Spirit – are called to share the living reality of the resurrected Messiah with the Jewish people, and by the mercy and grace of God, provoke them to spiritual jealousy.**

It is my deep hope and passionate prayer that God will bring His true Church to such a level of spiritual maturity that their testimony will break the ancient walls of Jewish resistance to and rejection of their Messiah, Jesus.

I believe that little by little, in many different ways and through many diverse methods and ministries, God will begin to release the Jewish people from the *"spirit of blindness"* that He put on them (John 12:37-40; Romans 11:7-10, 25). God put those "blinders" on and He can and will take them off! I believe that He will use those anointed and obedient servants as the vehicle by which blinder-removing revelation can come. The Bible promises us that individual Jews who respond to the *"ministry of reconciliation"* (2 Corinthians 5:18-20) and turn to the Lord will have that *"veil of blindness"* removed (2 Corinthians 3:14-16; Jeremiah 29:12, 13).

The Scriptures also promise us that there will come a time called the *"fullness of the Gentiles,"* when the Body of Christ comes to a particular level of spiritual maturity (Romans 11:25-26) the *"partial hardening"* of the hearts of the Jewish people toward their Messiah will be completely removed and *"all Israel will be saved."* This is also what the prophet Zechariah saw in the Spirit. In Chapter 12 verse 10, God said that He will *"pour out on the house of David and on the inhabitants of Jerusalem, the Spirit of grace and of supplication, so that they will look on Me whom they have pierced; and they will mourn for Him, as one mourns for an only son, and they will weep bitterly over Him like the bitter weeping over a firstborn."*

Not only were the Jews blinded to their Messiah, but because of the hatred and persecution the Jews suffered in the Name of Jesus, demonic spirits of anti-Christ were incorporated into the very fabric of Jewish identity.

These spirits have convinced the Jewish people that they could believe anything, everything, or nothing and remain part of the Jewish community – except believing that Jesus is the Messiah. These demons taught – and the Jewish people accepted it as truth – that if a Jew believed that Jesus is God's Divine Messiah and was baptized, that belief turned a Jew into a "Christian," which means that he/she is a heretic, an apostate, an idolater, and above all a "non-Jew." The Israeli Supreme Court made this belief the law of the land. On December 26, 1989, they ruled that Messianic Jews are no longer Jews, but are "Christians" and are therefore not eligible for Israeli citizenship under the Law of Return.

(It is interesting to note here that pre-Christian Jewish beliefs included the understanding of a Divine Messiah. God would, in fact, appear in human form – see Isaiah 7:14, 9:6; Jeremiah 23:5-6; Psalm 110:1).

The idea that faith in Jesus turns a Jew into a "non-Jew" is absurd, as are all doctrines of demons once you really examine them. The simple truth is that one's beliefs do not affect one's ethnicity. The descendants of Abraham remain his descendants regardless of what they believe. People's beliefs do not affect their DNA! You have today, as you did in Jesus' day, Jews who believe many diverse things about

CHAPTER 1 – A SEASON OF RESTORATION

God, the Torah and Judaism. These beliefs range from the ultra-orthodox to radical atheists, yet they are all considered Jews by the Jewish community. To claim citizenship in Israel, you have to prove your ancestry, not pass a belief test, except when it comes to believing in Jesus. Again, Messianic Jews have been denied Israeli citizenship.

So, we see that two major demonic entities, anti-Semitism and anti-Christ, working in tandem, have formed an effective three-fold strategy:

> **First** - they work to keep the Church separated from her "Jewish Roots" and antagonistic towards the Jewish people.
> **Second** - they work through this separated and antagonistic Church to keep an authentic faith-producing testimony of Jesus away from the Jews.
> **Third** - using these two strategies, they continue to hinder the Jewish people from believing in their own Messiah.

I believe that God has strategies to defeat this tandem and destroy its work. We must take the spiritual responsibility to intercede for the Church and the Jewish people. We must take authority over these two major demonic principalities. They have exercised great influence in the Church and among the Jewish people for millennia. This is an intense and strenuous spiritual battle. Only a determined and anointed people, who understand the nature of spiritual warfare and their spiritual authority, will win it.

The "tares" of anti-Semitism, with its fruit of suffering and death, only resulted in the continual hardening of the Jewish heart toward Jesus. That demonically inspired hatred enabled the spirit of anti-Christ to ingrain itself in the Jewish consciousness; I believe the opposite is true. The Love of the Church, in the Name of Jesus, can defeat that demonic principality and eradicate its influence in the hearts and minds of the Jewish people.

The "wheat" is getting free from the historical influences of those "tares." God is raising up a new generation with *His* heart, *His* love, and *His* power. The Holy Spirit is moving in the hearts of God's people, inspiring and empowering them to repent and renounce any influences, past or present, of anti-Semitism. They are bearing the fruit of that repentance in heartfelt prayer and ministering both to and on behalf of the Jewish people.

My prayer is that a loving, mature, unified, apostolic and prophetic Church, moving in a miracle-working anointing, will be the ultimate fruit of this freedom. Not only will such a Church be a jealousy-provoking witness to the Jewish people, but also the glorious Bride made ready for her Heavenly Groom! (Ephesians 5:27).

A Prophetic Vision

I see the Lord moving through His Body in dramatic, unprecedented, and profound ways. It will seem like an international "tsunami" of believers overflowing Israel and Jewish communities around the world with acts of repentance, love, and kindness, plus undeniable demonstrations of the power of the Kingdom of God. Accompanying this "tidal wave" will be indisputable testimonies of lives changed by Jesus the Messiah. This will be the message coming from the Body of Christ to the Jewish people:

> *"Your Messiah has changed our lives. Your God has become our God, and He has filled us with His great love for you. We are impelled by that love to proclaim the truth that changed our lives and set us free. Jesus is your Messiah!"*

If Jewish people respond with "Jesus is not our Messiah," we should tell them that God did not promise a Messiah to any other nation besides Israel. Only the Jews received such a promise. There is no such thing as a "Gentile Messiah" or a "Messiah for the Gentiles." Either Jesus/Yeshua is the Jewish Messiah, or He is not the Messiah at all!

By way of a practical strategy, what do you think the response of the Jewish world would be if it were flooded with testimonies of the reality of Jesus in the lives of individual believers from around the world? What would happen if every week or every month, believers from around the world sent an email, a text, tweet, blog post, or even a letter (remember them?) to the Chief Rabbi of Israel, or the local Rabbi or Jewish leader in their city, or to the many Jewish publications and websites, testifying to them of what the Messiah of Israel did in their life? What would the response of the Jewish community be to hearing what "their Messiah," the despised and rejected Jesus, was doing in the lives of millions of Gentile Christians around the world?

What if the testimonies enclosed a small love gift to support new immigrants to Israel, or various Jewish or Israeli charities, or for the defense of the land of Israel, or for building a hospital, or even a Synagogue? Christians building Synagogues instead of burning them! What a novel twist to history that would be! My prayer is that their response would be one of increasing curiosity and interest in investigating the claims of Jesus and the New Testament. May God open their hearts to a supernatural impartation of revelation faith so that they would come to know that Jesus/Yeshua is their long sought for Messianic King!

I believe that God desires to use many individuals, ministries, and Churches around the world to fulfill this vision and be such a "heart opening" witness.

God's Love for the Nations

Because God loves the world and is not willing that any should perish (2 Peter 3:9), we are also called to love, pray for, and testify to all nations, especially those hostile to the Jews, about God's purposes for them, as well as God's purposes for the Jewish people and the land of Israel.

As the Body of Christ is restored to her Biblical relationship and responsibility to the Jewish people, we must understand our mandate to stand with the Jews against their enemies. As witnesses for the Messiah and as part of our prophetic mantle, the Body of Christ is called, equipped and anointed to testify to Israel's enemies about the plans and purposes of the God of Israel as revealed in the Scriptures. This is also a part of fulfilling "the great commission" (Mark 16:15; Romans 16:25-26). It is no coincidence that the majority of the "10-40 window" of unevangelized nations is under the sway of the spirit of Islam. There are 865 million Muslims who live in that part of the world. The spirit of Islam is a major demonic principality that actively opposes the purposes of God for the nation of Israel and the Jewish people.

Those who make themselves the enemies of the Jewish people must understand that by being Israel's enemy, they are also making themselves the enemies of Israel's God. Those Muslims who fight against Israel, and against America for its support of Israel, are motivated by both religious beliefs and political ambition. They are focused not only on the destruction of the state of Israel, but their ultimate goal is the Islamization of the world. Because of the demonic spiritual realities that are behind their beliefs, we must pray for the Muslims, love them, and testify to them of the truth of the Gospel.

We must also proclaim to them the Biblical revelations and prophetic declarations that God has made to the Jewish people. We must explain to them that God owns the land of Israel (Leviticus 25:23), and the city of Jerusalem (1 Kings 11:36). God has covenanted that land and that city to the Jewish people as an eternal inheritance (Leviticus 20:24; Isaiah 60:21). Because this is a spiritual battle, only the Holy Spirit can reveal the truth of these verses to them. Until He does, we must continue to pray and proclaim God's Word.

The Bible clearly says that, *"Those who curse Israel will be cursed, and those who bless Israel will be blessed"* (Genesis 12:3). History has proven this over and over again. All of Israel's ancient enemies are gone, and Israel lives! Haman, Nebuchadnezzar, Pharaoh, and their kind are all gone, and Israel lives! Those kings, popes, bishops, preachers, inquisitors, and their kind who sought Israel's demise are all gone, yet Israel lives! Hitler, the Nazis, Stalin and the Communists are gone, and Israel lives! Hussein and Arafat are gone, and Israel lives! Hamas, Hezbollah, the Islamic Brotherhood, Al-Qaeda, ISIS, Ayatollahs and all those who hate Israel will be gone, and Israel will live! The Scriptures make it clear that Israel is an eternal nation whose King will rule and reign over the whole earth from Israel's capital city, Jerusalem (Jeremiah 31:31-37; Zechariah 14:7-9, 11; Ezekiel 37:24; 1 Kings 11:13).

Again, by way of practical strategy, what would the response of the Muslim world be if millions of Christians around the world similarly flooded them with testimonies of Jesus and then humbly and lovingly affirmed that the land of Israel, and the city of Jerusalem, belongs to the Jews (Leviticus 25:23; Psalm 132:13-14) because the God of the Christians and the Jews has declared it to be so in His Holy Scriptures.

The Koran in Surah 29:46 teaches Muslims to respect the Bible. My prayer is that they would be deeply challenged to re-examine what they now believe, read the Bible for themselves, come to faith in Jesus, and love the Jewish people. I believe that one of God's end time strategies is to turn Muslims into Christians who love Jews!

An explosion of support of this kind would be a tremendous testimony and a great source of comfort to the Jewish people. The world press would certainly take notice of it, especially if the flood of correspondence jammed up the international lines of communication. Can you imagine the leaders of the world asking the international Christian community to please stop all the texts, emails, social media posts and letters because we were overloading the internet? That would be a day of great victory for the Kingdom of God! Lord make it so, Amen!

CHAPTER 2 – AN APPOINTED TIME FOR HEALING LOVE, WHY NOW?

In December of 1990, I had a profound encounter with the Lord in prayer. He spoke very clearly into my spirit of His intention to reconcile the Church to her "Jewish Roots" and to the Jewish people. These were the exact words He said:

> "I intend to accomplish Four Reconciliations:
> 1. I intend to reconcile the Church to her 'Jewish Roots.'
> 2. I intend to reconcile the Church to the Jewish people.
> 3. I intend to reconcile the Jewish people to their Messiah, and
> 4. I intend to reconcile the Messiah to planet Earth."

Immediately after He spoke this, He began to show me these four reconciliations in various Scriptures. It was a life-changing experience as I felt in some small way what it must have been like for the two disciples on the road to Emmaus to have the Messiah open the Scriptures to them (Luke 24:32). This happened very early in the morning, and later I shared with my wife Janet what the Lord said. We began to pray and fast about what this meant and what we were to do about it.

During one afternoon of prayer, we both had independent visions about the spiritual warfare we were going to encounter. I had a vision of the two of us in a small boat in the ocean with a huge storm coming our way. In the vision, I heard the Lord say to me, "Raise your sails and sail into the storm." I replied, "Lord, the Bible says that *when a wise man sees trouble coming, he hides himself*" (Proverbs 22:3, 27:12). My quoting the Scriptures did not change His mind. He said again, "Lift up your sails; you are heading into a storm." At the same time that I saw this, Janet saw herself being escorted by Jesus down a long staircase into a very dark place, which she realized was Hell. Then she saw what looked like a gym where extremely huge muscular demonic creatures were working out. "Who are they?" she asked. Jesus answered, "They are the demonic spirits that fight against anyone who works on behalf of God's purposes for Israel and the Jewish people. They will be coming after you and Howard."

A short time later, we entered that storm and faced those demonic forces. We encountered one of the greatest spiritual battles we ever experienced. It affected every aspect of our lives: family, health, finances, ministry relationships, etc. Because we set our hearts to obey the Lord, we eventually came through victoriously. Through that intense battle, we learned many things and gained much insight and understanding into the demonic nature of this conflict. Over the years we have been able to help others who have heard the call of the Lord to labor on behalf of God's prophetic purposes for Israel and the Jewish people. In fact, we have found that this battle unfolds in the lives of virtually everyone who joins in this move of the Spirit. If you are encountering new levels of demonic resistance, please do not be discouraged and don't take it personally. It is not about you! It just means that you are moving forward, going through the *"gates of the enemy"* and taking ground for the Kingdom of God (Matthew 16:18; Ephesians 6:10-18; 2 Corinthians 4:1-18).

Psalm 102:13-18

One of the key Scriptures the Lord opened to me was Psalm 102:13-18.

> *"You will arise and have compassion on Zion; for it is time to be gracious to her, for the appointed time has come. Surely Your servants find pleasure in her stones and feel pity for her dust. So the nations will fear the name of the LORD and all the kings of the earth Your glory. For the LORD has built up Zion; He has appeared in His glory. He has regarded the prayer of the destitute and has not despised their prayer. This will be written for the generation to come, that a people yet to be created may praise the LORD."*

CHAPTER 2 – AN APPOINTED TIME FOR HEALING LOVE, WHY NOW?

We begin to understand these extremely significant verses by looking at verse 18 first. Most English Bibles translate verse 18 to read "a generation to come, or a future generation." These are not accurate translations. The Hebrew word, אַחֲרוֹן, (*ah-cha-rown,*) is translated as "future" but should be translated "end," "last," or "final." It should read "last or final generation." In other words, when we see the previous verses coming to pass, we can know that we are in the "last days" because as the text says, this is written for the "*ah-cha-rown.*"

To understand these verses or even the entire concept of the "last days," you must first understand the context in which God is relating to the nation of Israel. We read about this in the Hebrew Scriptures. In the Torah (the first five books of the Bible), we learn the story of God's covenant with Israel. God made covenantal promises to the patriarchs, Abraham, Isaac, and Jacob, and after delivering the Israelites from slavery in Egypt, He entered into covenant relationship with them as a nation at Mount Sinai. Through the ministry of Moses, God gave them His Torah (literally "Instructions") and His commandments ("Mitzvot"). In the Torah, God declared the conditions of the covenant. He told the Jewish people that if they kept His commandments they would be blessed *"above all the people on the earth"* (Deuteronomy 7:14), and He would give them *"His land forever"* (Genesis 13:15, 17:8, 48:4; Exodus 32:13; 2 Chronicles 20:7; Ezra 9:12; Isaiah 60:21; Jeremiah 7;7, 17:4; Ezekiel 37:25).

Please pay special attention to the fact that **the land of Israel belongs to God!** It does not belong to the Jews, or the Arabs, or anyone else (Leviticus 25:23; 2 Chronicles 7:20; Ezekiel 38:16; Joel 3:2). God warned the Jewish people that if they disobeyed His Torah and broke His commandments, they would be cursed. Part of that curse would be their expulsion from the land of Israel and their scattering and persecution among the nations (Leviticus 26; Deuteronomy 28). However, God repeatedly promised through His prophets that He would never break His covenant with the Jewish people (Judges 2;1; Genesis 17:7-8), or allow them to be annihilated (for example see Jeremiah 30:11, 31:35-37).

Psalm 102:13 is one of many verses that teach us that in the *"final generation,"* or at the *"end of the age,"* God Himself will rise up and have *"mercy (or compassion) on Zion"* and re-gather them to their land and ultimately to *"David their King"* (Isaiah 43:5, 54:7; Jeremiah 30:3, 9, 31:10, 32:37; Ezekiel 20:34, 34:13, 23-24, 36:24-28, 37:24-25; Hosea 3:5; Amos 9:15).

This expression, *"mercy or compassion on Zion,"* is what I call a "prophetic clue." We, as "spiritual detectives," must understand the "prophetic clues" given to us in the Scriptures. Proverbs 25:2 says that *"it is the glory of God to hide a matter, and the glory of kings to search it out."* Since we are presently seated in Heavenly places with the King (Ephesians 2:6), and are called ultimately to sit on His throne with Him (Revelation 3:21) and are commanded to *"search the Scriptures"* (John 5:39), we have the authority to be those "spiritual detectives." Searching for those clues and their meaning gives us the opportunities to receive the necessary spiritual understanding and insight into the days in which we are living and what the will of God is for us as we endeavor to truly *"know the Lord and do exploits"* for Him (Daniel 11:32).

After the destruction of the Temple in 70 AD, the Jews who were still in Israel were scattered to the four corners of the earth and for the next almost 1900 years suffered much persecution and bloodshed. God in His sovereignty determined the boundaries of their scattering and their suffering. He did not allow them to be exterminated in the Holocaust, and in 1948 God began to have compassion upon His ancient people. Out of the ashes of the death camps, the modern state of Israel was born. The international regathering of the Jewish people began.

Overcoming all natural odds, this vastly outnumbered fledgling nation of war-ravaged death-camp survivors, and early Zionist pioneers defeated the combined armed forces of the surrounding Arab nations. Slowly the land was reclaimed, and prophecies began to be fulfilled. The desert began to *"bloom like a rose"* (Isaiah 35:1-2). It is true that those who returned were mostly secular socialists, not repenting believers, but their heart was turned toward Zion (Psalm 84:5). A *"door of hope in the valley of trouble was opened"* (Hosea 2:15). Jews from many nations began to return to the land, and that return continues to this day.

CHAPTER 2 – AN APPOINTED TIME FOR HEALING LOVE, WHY NOW?

In June of 1967, Israel fought the famous "Six Day War" and was once again victorious over multinational Arab armies. (Do you see the "clue" here: What else happened in only six days?) During those six days, Israel not only decisively defeated her enemies, she nearly doubled her land size, and even more significantly, fulfilled one of the major end-time prophecies that Jesus Himself proclaimed in Luke 21:24. He declared that *"Jerusalem will be trampled under foot by the Gentiles until the times of the Gentiles are fulfilled."* For the first time since 70 AD, the Jewish people had governmental sovereignty over the city of Jerusalem, including the Temple Mount.

The leaders of Israel at that time understood all too well the political and religious significance of the Temple Mount for the international Islamic world with its Dome of the Rock shrine and Al-Aqsa Mosque. Seeking to circumvent the hatred of hundreds of millions of Muslims around the world, they immediately returned authority over the Temple Mount to the Islamic leaders. Having just won a tremendous victory, Israel did not want to start an international holy war.

Jerusalem and the area around the Temple Mount remained under Jewish rule. This is a very important sign of the times and a significant clue about the days in which we live. Could it be that the *"times of the Gentiles"* began to come to an end in 1967, and we began to move into a new season that we can call "the times of the Jews?" I believe so! Most Christians are unaware of the fact that after June of 1967, the Holy Spirit began to move around the earth revealing to young Jewish men and women that Jesus/Yeshua is the Jewish Messiah. If you look at the Body of Christ today, you will find that the vast majority of Jewish believers and ministry leaders came to faith in Yeshua after June of 1967.

There are more Jewish leaders in the Body of Christ now than at any time since the first century. Before June of 1967, there were few Messianic Jewish congregations in the world, and perhaps one or two in Israel. According to reports from various sources today, there are approximately 150 indigenous Hebrew-speaking Messianic congregations in Israel as well as hundreds of other Messianic congregations around the world. Additionally, there are many ministries teaching the "Jewish Roots" of Christian faith. This is another testimony to the season the Church is in. Of course, the *"times of the Gentiles"* are certainly not over. The Gospel has not yet permeated all the nations of the world as it must before Jesus can return (Matthew 24:14; Mark 13:10). But God is moving on behalf of, and among, the Jewish people, just as He is in the nations of the world.

Psalm 102:14 declares that when God begins to have mercy on the Jewish people, something begins to happen to the Body of Christ. The text says that God's *"servants will have compassion on Zion's stones and feel pity for her dust."* On the day that the Lord opened these verses to me, He told me that the servants spoken of here are His authentic disciples. They are the ones who only want to do His will as His faithful and obedient servants. Since 1991, I have been privileged to witness thousands of believers respond to God's healing love for Israel and the Jewish people as the Holy Spirit reveals the Father's heart to them.

Christians from every nation are having *"compassion on Zion's stones"* as they respond to that revelation. They are reaching out in prayer and diverse ways of expressing that compassion to Israel, understanding that *Zion's stones* refer to living Jewish people, not rocks and ancient huge stone blocks. They are also feeling *"pity for her dust"* as they learn the horrific history of "Christian" anti-Semitism. They recognize that the dust spoken of here refers to Jewish people who were persecuted and killed in the Name of Jesus. We continually see meetings where true disciples are expressing deep remorse for the sins of the Church toward the Jewish people. They are renouncing the demonic spirits that inspired that persecution and are demonstrating their repentance by standing with the Jewish people and the nation of Israel. (If you are unfamiliar with the horrific history of "Christian" anti-Semitism, please read my book, "So Deeply Scarred." It is a small book giving a very concise overview of that painful story.)

Standing with God's purposes for Israel and the Jewish people can often come at a great price and individuals can often face the anti-Semitism that remains in many churches and ministries. We know many people who have been "excommunicated" from their churches and even from some families because they chose to stand with the Jewish people. They understand that the price they pay to stand with

CHAPTER 2 – AN APPOINTED TIME FOR HEALING LOVE, WHY NOW?

God for the fulfillment of His present prophetic purposes is insignificant compared to the glory and honor they bring to the Lord and will share in on the great "Day of Judgement" (2 Corinthians 4:16-17; Romans 8:18).

In further fulfillment of verse 14 of Psalm 102, as believers receive revelation about God's heart and purposes for Israel and the Jewish people, they are inspired to learn more about the "Jewish Roots" of their faith. Since 1990, there has been a growing worldwide movement within the Body of Christ to learn about their Biblical "Jewish Roots" and the restoration of their relationship and responsibility to the Jewish people. Before 1990, there were a few scattered ministries involved in this work. Now there are hundreds. Before 1990, very few Christians thought about the "Jewish Roots" of the Christian faith. It just wasn't taught.

Today, however, it is not unusual at all to find people in every part of the Body of Christ learning about, and teaching, these truths and expressing them in some form or another. Churches around the world are learning Hebraic forms of worship and praise; they are blowing Shofars, wearing prayer shawls, learning about the prophetic significance of the Feasts of the Lord (Leviticus 23), and celebrating those Feasts in a New Covenant context. They are discovering the spiritual riches of the Torah, the "Jewishness" of Jesus and the beliefs and practices of the original Messianic congregations. They understand God's prophetic purposes for the Body of Christ and the Jewish people and the end time significance of the restoration of that relationship (Ephesians 2:11-22; Romans 11).

Psalm 102 continues to open for us an understanding that as God has *"mercy on Zion"* and His servants follow His example, something wonderful happens in all of the nations of the earth. Verse 15 tells us, *"The nations will fear the name of the Lord and all the kings of the earth your glory."* As you follow the history of worldwide evangelism, you can see that after the establishment of the modern state of Israel in 1948, there was a parallel increase in international missionary work that continues to this day. In fact, there is more global ministry going on now than at any time since the original outpouring of the Holy Spirit on the Day of Pentecost in Acts chapter 2! This follows the pattern Paul reveals in Romans 1:16, and 2:9-10, *"To the Jew first, then to the nations."* As God has mercy on Zion, so He also has mercy on all people. As God turns His heart of compassion on Israel, so He also does to the whole earth.

Here is something to keep your eyes on as we watch the *"signs of the times"* (Matthew 16:3). It is important to recognize that there is a very close parallel between what God does with natural Israel and what He does in the Church. Here are a few examples:

In the same year that Columbus discovered America, 1492, the Jews were expelled from Spain. Within that same generation, the printing press was invented (1450) which started the process of making the Bible available to everyone and Martin Luther nailed his famous 95 theses to the door of the Wittenberg Castle Church, sparking the Protestant Reformation (1517). In the 1890's and early 1900's, there was a parallel between major outpourings of the Holy Spirit upon the Body of Christ and the emergence of modern Zionism. At the same general time that Theodor Herzl was birthing the Zionist movement and proclaiming that Israel would become a nation once again, there were major outpourings of the Holy Spirit in the Church. The Pentecostal movement began in the United States as did the famous Welsh Revival. Both of those outpourings changed the Church forever, even as the movement for the eventual establishment of the state of Israel changed the history of the Jews and the world.

The Charismatic Renewal, which has powerfully influenced both Catholics and Protestants around the world, began in 1967, the same year that Jerusalem came under Jewish sovereignty, and God began to bring many young Jewish people to faith in the Messiah. The "Jewish Roots" movement began in earnest in the early 1990's, the same time the first Gulf war started, and the Internet began its major public expansion. Daniel 12:4 identifies the expansion of knowledge and travel as one of the signs of the *"end times."* Both are expanding at phenomenal rates.

Consider also the increase of spiritual activity in the world as the Gospel spreads at unparalleled rates in Africa, South America, and Asia.

CHAPTER 2 – AN APPOINTED TIME FOR HEALING LOVE, WHY NOW?

Islam is also growing rapidly, as is its terrorist offspring. At the same time, missionaries are reporting that Muslims are coming to faith in Jesus in unprecedented numbers. Religion is at the forefront of politics around the world, and interest in the person of Jesus is increasing. We see Him and religious issues at the forefront of almost daily news coverage. We are also witnessing the continuing box office success of Biblically themed movies.

These parallels and interconnections between significant events taking place in Israel, in the Body of Christ and the world, constitute more "prophetic clues" to what God is doing in our generation. But be careful how you understand and interpret these "signs." There were those in previous generations who interpreted events to mean that Jesus would return in their time. They made bad decisions because of their misunderstanding. Jesus said that one of the hallmarks of the end of the age would be rampant deception (Matthew 24:4-5). We must be very cautious as we seek to follow the leading of the Holy Spirit in the days ahead (1 Thessalonians 5:19-21).

In summary, Psalm 102:13-15 outlines three prophetic events we are now watching come to pass:

(1) God is having mercy on Zion.
(2) The Church is returning to her "Jewish Roots" and to her Biblical relationship and responsibility to the Jewish people.
(3) World evangelism is increasing.

I believe that verse 16 is one of the most powerful revelatory verses in the entire Bible because it shows us the direct connection between those three events and the second coming of Jesus. It ties the three previous verses together in such a way as to show us that these three moves of God are part and parcel of what He means by the expression *"builds up Zion."* What happens when God finishes this process of building up Zion? He makes this most amazing declaration in verse 16:

"He will appear in His Glory!!"

This is nothing less than the literal return of Jesus!!!

Is it any wonder the devil so fiercely fights everything and anything that relates to God's purposes for the Church and the Jewish people?

CHAPTER 3 – SATAN'S MASTER PLAN TO PREVENT THE RETURN OF JESUS

Satan has a long history of trying to prevent the fulfillment of God's plans and purposes. He attempted to take God's throne from Him, but was cast out from Heaven (Isaiah 14:12-15). He deceived Adam and Eve only to hear his doom prophesied when God spoke the first Messianic prophecy which declared that his head would be bruised by the seed of the woman (Genesis 3:15). He tried to keep the Jewish people in slavery, but God sent Moses to set His people free (Exodus 3). He sought to prevent the Jewish people from entering and conquering the Promised Land, but all their enemies were defeated (Psalm 78:54-55). Balaam's attempts at cursing Israel so that Balak could defeat them were turned into a declaration of blessings (Numbers 22:12; Deuteronomy 23:5).

A demonic prince tried to stop the prophet Daniel from receiving major Messianic prophecies and end-time revelations but was not successful (Daniel 10:12-14). The devil sought to end both the life of Moses and Jesus in infancy by slaughtering innocent children (Exodus 1:16; Matthew 2:16). He attempted to destroy the ministry of Jesus before it began with the temptations in the wilderness (Matthew 4:1-11). When Peter tried to hinder Jesus from going to the cross, Jesus identified the spirit that was influencing him and addressed Satan directly in His rebuke of Peter (Matthew 16:23). Satan hindered Paul when he wanted to be with the Thessalonians (1 Thessalonians 2:18). Paul also warned us not to be ignorant of the devil's methods as he seeks to thwart God's purposes in our lives (2 Corinthians 2:11).

The devil knows that when Jesus returns he will be utterly defeated and destroyed. He will be bound for a thousand years and ultimately thrown into the Lake of Fire (Revelation 20:2-3, 10). Because of this, he has historically used and presently continues to use, every kind of strategy and tactic he can to prevent the return of the Messiah. But all of his attempts are in vain because God is ultimately sovereign over the world (Job 42:2; Psalm 33:10-11, 103:19; Daniel 4:34-35; Ephesians 1:10-11). The Word of God cannot fail (Isaiah 40:8, 55:11; Matthew 24:35; 1 Peter 1:25). The coming of the King of Kings is as *"certain as the dawn"* (Hosea 6:1-3; see also Psalm 96:13, 98:9, 102:1-6; Micah 1:3-4; Zechariah 2:10; 1 Thessalonians 4:15-17).

In Acts 3:21, Peter proclaimed a pivotal part of God's plan for the return of the Messiah. The Holy Spirit revealed that Jesus would *"remain in Heaven until the time for the restoration of all things that the prophets have spoken."* Satan, who always listens when the Word of God is preached so he can steal it (Matthew 13:18; Mark 4:15), heard this prophetic message and conceived a plan that he thought would keep Jesus in heaven forever. If he could somehow cause the failure of the prophets' words, Jesus would never be able to return, and his present influence over humanity would continue forever (Matthew 4:8; 1 John 5:19). He understood clearly what Peter was prophesying. If the words of the prophets do not come to pass, Jesus can never return and destroy him and his demonic empire.

Allow me to repeat this central truth; the Bible is very clear in its declaration that the *"Scriptures cannot be broken"* (John 10:35). It is *"forever settled in Heaven"* (Psalm 119:89) and *"God's purposes will be established, He will accomplish all His good pleasure"* (Isaiah 46:10). Jesus said that everything written in the Hebrew Scriptures would be fulfilled (Matthew 5:18). He also said that His own words were eternal, thereby asserting His deity. *"Heaven and earth shall pass away, but My words will never pass away"* (Matthew 24:35; Mark 13:31; Luke 21:33). Foretelling the future through the mouths of His prophets and then bringing it to pass, is one of the ways the God of Israel proves that He, and only He, is the one true God (Isaiah 41:22-23, 45:21). God's Word will be fulfilled! His plans will come to pass!

So, what did the prophets speak? What are the divine prophecies and promises whose fulfillment Satan so desperately seeks to thwart? The essential message of the Hebrew Scriptures is that God entered into a covenant with the Jewish people. He brought them, as a nation, into a relationship with Himself (Deuteronomy 4:7). He gave them His land, the land of Israel as an everlasting inheritance (Leviticus 25:23; 2 Chronicles 7:20; Ezekiel 38:16; Joel 1:6, 3:2). Through His servant

CHAPTER 3 – SATAN'S MASTER PLAN TO PREVENT THE RETURN OF JESUS

Moses, God told the Jewish people that the penalty for their disobedience to His commandments would be exile from the land, international dispersion, and great suffering among the *"goyim"* – the Gentiles (Leviticus 26; Deuteronomy 28).

But Moses, as well as the prophets God repeatedly sent to the Jewish people, also declared that God would not allow His covenant people to be destroyed (Deuteronomy 30:1-10; Jeremiah 31:35-37). God promised that in the last days, at the end of this age, He will have compassion upon the scattered and persecuted children of Israel and regather them back to their land and to "David" their King. (Psalm 102:13; Deuteronomy 30; Hosea 3:5; Jeremiah 30:9; Ezekiel 37:24). "David" here is a reference to Jesus, King David's greatest descendant, the Messianic King whom God promised would sit upon David's throne forever (1 Chronicles 17:11-14).

The devil is seeking to prevent the fulfillment of these prophecies by dividing the land of Israel and creating a sovereign Palestinian state, which he would then try to use to destroy the nation of Israel. If he can do that, the Jews would have no land to return to, the prophetic Scriptures would fail, and Jesus would not be able to return.

He understands that the present regathering of the Jewish people to the land of Israel is part of the *"restoration of all things"* spoken of in Acts 3:21. He understands very well what will happen to him when the words of the prophets are fulfilled and Messiah Jesus returns! All of the demons in the world know this, and fear it, as they should (Matthew 8:29). When Messiah returns, the devil and all of the demons with him will be bound for a thousand years (Revelation 20:2-3) and then thrown into the Lake of Fire where they will be tormented forever and ever (Revelation 20:10).

From my studies of the Scriptures and research of Jewish history, as well as my own experiences with God as a Jewish believer in Yeshua, I have come to understand that Satan has devised two main strategies in his attempts to stop the words of the prophets from coming to pass and thereby prevent the Messiah from returning.

Strategy #1:

A) Kill all the Jews.

If Satan could succeed in killing all the Jewish people, there obviously would be no one for God to regather to the land of Israel. That would cause the words of the prophets to fail and Jesus would have to remain in Heaven. Throughout history, Satan has often sought opportunities to kill the Jewish people. This, of course, is what he attempted to complete in the Holocaust. Hitler's ascendance to power was a manifestation of raw satanic power and deception. How else is it possible to explain his rise from obscurity to absolute dictatorial power over life and death or his incredible ability to mesmerize an entire country and turn vast numbers of "cultured people" into cold blooded murderers dedicated to the systematic extermination of every single Jewish man, woman, and child.

The satanic roots of Nazism become apparent when you realize that their doctrines were deeply entrenched in the occult. One of their occult beliefs was that the world was once ruled by a race of "Aryan Supermen," from whom the German people descended. These "Aryan Supermen" were physically perfect and had various kinds of mystical powers, like telepathy. Because these "Aryans" mixed their blood with inferior races, particularly the Jews, they lost their superhuman abilities, and the world was plunged into darkness. If the German people could purge themselves of the blood of inferior races, then their original "Aryan blood" could be restored, and they would once again regain those powers and take their rightful place as the rulers of the world. This would usher in a thousand years of true peace, harmony, and prosperity. Believing this was one reason that mass murder was so easy for them.

The present fanatical Islamic goal to destroy the nation of Israel and "drive the Jews into the sea" is the latest manifestation of Satan's attempt to nullify the Scriptures. Fanatical Islamic anti-Semitism is not fundamentally a hatred of the nation of Israel and the Jewish people, although that is what individuals might be thinking and feeling. Hiding behind the guise of radical Islamic doctrines and political ideologies are demonic spirits attempting to prevent the return of Jesus!

CHAPTER 3 – SATAN'S MASTER PLAN TO PREVENT THE RETURN OF JESUS

These demons launched a war against the establishment of the nation of Israel in 1948, and they are the driving force behind all of Israel's wars and terror attacks.

The Scripture declares that Jesus, who was, and still is, rejected by the vast majority of Jewish people, must be received by them (Zechariah 12:10-11; Romans 11:15). The Jewish people must invite Him to return. They must say to Him, *"Baruch HaBa B'shem Adonai"- Blessed is He who comes in the name of the Lord"* (Matthew 23:39) before He will physically return to the Mount of Olives (Zechariah 14:4) and set up His International Kingdom headquarters in Jerusalem (Isaiah 2:14). If Israel is destroyed or if there are no Jews alive to repent of their national unbelief and receive the rejected Messiah, the words of the prophets and the promises of God would have failed, and the Lord Jesus would be unable to return.

B) Assimilate the Jews

As with any people group that is living as a minority within a foreign culture, the Jewish people were, and in many aspects still are, living under pressure to become like the people they live among. What has been different about the Jews is the fact that they were historically put under uniquely intense coercive pressures to abandon their ancient covenant faith, reject their ethnic identity as Jews, and "convert" to the religion of "Christianity." This would, in effect, mean that they would become Gentiles. Failing to kill the Jewish people, assimilation is a choice that Satan will accept because if there are no people who would identify themselves as Jews, the Scriptures regarding them would similarly fail to be fulfilled, and Jesus would not be able to return. Messianic Judaism is a prophetic response to this pressure. It gives Jewish people an opportunity to live and identify themselves as Jews, while believing in their Messiah, Jesus.

If Church leaders, who in their ignorance and pride, were behind those pressures to compel the Jews to reject their ethnic and national identity by forced conversion and cultural assimilation, had possessed even a basic understanding of what the Apostle Paul taught in Romans 11, they would never have acted in arrogance toward the Jewish people. They would have understood the revelation God gave to that great

Jewish apostle in that amazing chapter. It was the plan of God for the Jewish rejection of Jesus to be the means by which the Gentiles would inherit the spiritual riches of Messiah's salvation, and then for those same Gentiles to demonstrate those riches as a testimony to stir the Jewish people to spiritual jealousy.

Instructed by *"doctrines of demons"* and inflamed to hatred by the *"activities of evil spirits,"* (1 Timothy 4:1) the Church was manipulated into repeated persecution of the Jews. Instead of inspiring the Jewish people to faith in their own Messiah, they drove them away from Him at the point of a sword. The Church's vicious hatred of the Jews caused the Jewish people to bond together in more intense ways to resist the enormous pressures to "convert" to the "religion" of their persecutors or to assimilate into their cultures.

In addition to the historical pressure to "convert" to "Christianity," there are also the more subtle and pervasive dynamics of normal assimilation. Over time, groups tend to melt into one another as generations intermarry and adopt the various cultural norms present in every society. It is a testimony to their supernatural calling and destiny that there are Jews who have maintained their distinct national identity during their almost two-thousand year banishment among the nations.

It is true that a percentage of Jews yielded to "forced conversion" rather than face martyrdom or expulsion and eventually lost all of their Jewish identity. We see throughout history that many sought to secretly keep some vestige of their "Jewishness" because they knew in their "heart of hearts" that they were still Jews. For example, during the horrors of the Spanish Inquisition, Jews who were forced to deny their Jewish identity were called by various names: Conversos, Crypto-Jews, New Christians or Marranos. They held onto the hope that if freedom was granted to them, they would be able to openly identify as Jews and practice their ancient religion.

Even though the Jews were exiled to so many different countries, each having their unique cultural dynamics, the Jewish people have always shared a unifying sense of peoplehood. Disagreeing on many issues,

CHAPTER 3 – SATAN'S MASTER PLAN TO PREVENT THE RETURN OF JESUS

(as evidenced by the famous Jewish quip, "two Jews, three opinions"), we observe that Jewish people have the same "spirit," the same "spiritual identity." This can be seen when Jewish people are faced with a presentation of the Gospel. Seeing "Christianity" as a foreign religion and a threat to their identity as "Jews," a typical Jewish response is, *"I was born a Jew, and I will die a Jew."*

This unifying identity is a supernatural phenomenon. The survival of the Jewish people as "a people" – even as a "remnant" (Deuteronomy 4:27, 28:62; Isaiah 1:9, 10:22, 11:11, 16; Jeremiah 23:3; Romans 9:27) – cannot be explained by mere sociological, religious or cultural reasons. None of these merely human factors would have enabled even this "remnant" to survive the continual and often horrific pressures to either perish or reject their Jewish identity and assimilate into the cultures and religions of their oppressors. Simply put, the Jewish people would have disappeared long ago.

To have survived their national exile, with the destruction of Jerusalem and their Temple in 70 AD, and kept for 2,000 years a "Jewish identity" with a basic set of common beliefs and practices, is evidence of the immutability of their national identity. It is a powerful testimony to the veracity and supernatural reality of the divine promises written in the Scriptures. The same God who *scattered* the Jews (Leviticus 26:33; Deuteronomy 4:27, 28:64; Jeremiah 9:16; Zechariah 7:14) declared that He would *regather* them (Deuteronomy 30:3-4; Jeremiah 30:11, 31:10; Hosea 3:4-5; Zechariah 8:7-8, 10:6) and fulfill His prophetic purposes for His ancient covenant people. He is doing this, and He will continue to do so!!

God *chose* the Jewish people (Deuteronomy 7:6-8; 1 Kings 3:8; Isaiah 41:8-9; Isaiah 44:1-2) and *called* them for specific purposes (Genesis 12:1-3, 22:18; Leviticus 19:6; Romans 3:2, 9:4-5). It is these purposes that make them a *Holy, (i.e. set apart)* people (Leviticus 11:45; 19:2; 20:26; Deuteronomy 7:6; 28:9; Isaiah 62:12; Romans 11:16). This does not mean that they were (or are) particularly righteous or pure (most were and are not). It means that they were (and still are) *set apart* to fulfill a unique calling and destiny (Exodus 19:5-6; Isaiah 2:2-6, 59:20-21; Micah 4:1-4; Matthew 23:39; Acts 3:21; Romans 11:15, 29).

Because of God's covenantal promises and purposes, the Jews as a people, and Israel as a nation, are *"beloved of God"* (Leviticus 26:42; Deuteronomy 7:8, 9:5, 10:15; 2 Kings 13:23; Romans 11:28). They have a *unique calling* (Exodus 19:5; Deuteronomy 7:6, 26:18), and are *eternal and indestructible* (Leviticus 26:44; Jeremiah 31:3, 35-37, 33:20; Romans 11:29). The calling and the purposes of God for the Jewish people are ultimately centered on the return of their Messianic King and the establishment of the Kingdom of God on the earth!

This does not mean that all Jews are guaranteed eternal salvation merely because of their ethnic identity. Everyone will face God's judgment. Some are trusting in their own righteousness and good works. Others are trusting in the forgiveness that Messiah's atoning death provided for them. God is the *"Righteous Judge"* (Genesis 18:25; Psalm 9:8, 96:13, 98:9; 2 Corinthians 5:10; 1 Peter 4:5) who decides who gets into His Heaven!

As the Scripture proclaims, Jews from the nations of the world are, and will continue to be, re-gathered to their ancient homeland. As we move closer to the return of the Lord, Jews from Western nations will be compelled to leave their comfortable lifestyles and return to the land of Israel. Their return may be prompted by outbreaks of violent anti-Semitism, or terrorist attacks, or war involving weapons of mass destruction (God forbid), or massive international financial collapse that creates global chaos, or by a phenomenal supernatural outpouring of the Holy Spirit (may it be Lord!). Perhaps it will be a combination of all or some of these, or something else. **What we do know is that God said it would happen** (Isaiah 11:11-12, 43:5-6, 54:7; Psalm 107:3; Hosea 3:4-5; Amos 9:14-15; Isaiah; Jeremiah 30:3; Ezekiel 37:21; Zechariah 8:7-8), **and it will. Watch for it! It will be a major sign of the imminence of the Lord's return!**

If Satan had succeeded in his attempts to assimilate the Jewish people, the result would have been the same as if he had managed to kill all of them. When the time came for the Lord to regather His people, there would be none who identified themselves as Jews. The words of the prophets would fail, and Jesus would remain in Heaven forever.

CHAPTER 3 – SATAN'S MASTER PLAN TO
PREVENT THE RETURN OF JESUS

Strategy #2:

Use the Church as an instrument of death and assimilation.

This dual strategy of death and assimilation represents the first aspect of Satan's plan to prevent the return of Jesus. The second part of his plan is even more insidious because it seeks to use the Church to prevent the return of her own Lord. This is the ultimate spiritual irony.

The true Church, made up of redeemed people from the nations of the earth, is called to live and love as the very Body of Christ. They are the people who are called to lovingly obey their Lord, do His will, and manifest His life, love, and power in the world. They are commanded to love their Lord, their neighbors, and even their enemies (Matthew 5:43-44). The Body of Christ is called to reflect Christ's love, character, holiness, faith, joy, and power by their words and deeds. Indeed, they are the people called to emulate and demonstrate the true person of Jesus the Messiah (2 Corinthians 5:20).

One of the most important, yet least understood and unfulfilled missions of the Church is to provoke natural Israel to spiritual jealousy (Romans 11:11, 14). The Apostle Paul recognized the prophetic significance of Deuteronomy 32:21 for the Church, when he made the clear declaration in Romans 10:19 that God intends to use the Gentile believers from the nations of the world, *"a people who are not a people,"* to fulfill that Scripture. Deuteronomy 32:21 also predicts that God would provoke the Jewish people to anger with a *"foolish nation."* The historic predominantly Gentile "Christian Church," influenced by demons, rejected its "Jewish Roots" and its Biblical relationship and responsibility to the Jewish people and became their tormentors. That demonized "Church" became that *"foolish nation"* and succeeded in provoking the Jewish people to anger.

How satanic and bitterly ironic it is that the Church, which was called to be the vehicle of redemptive love and the light of joyous salvation to the nations, became for the Jewish people an instrument of vile hatred, intense persecution, and murder. Creating the spiritual and cultural soil for the seeds of Nazism to take root, the anti-Semitic doctrines and practices of that "demonized Church" eventually led to the systematic murder of six million Jewish men, women, and children. The vicious and violent history of that demonic counterfeit "Church" toward the Jews has understandably created within the Jewish corporate consciousness an entrenched and pervasive mindset of rejection and hostility toward the "Christian religion" and its "founder" Jesus Christ, which this "Church" horrifically misrepresented.

A Connection Many Christians Fail to See

But God has a plan to bring the Jewish people to faith in the despised and rejected Jesus. The plan has never changed, and it will be fulfilled one day. Perhaps even in our lifetime! In Matthew 23:39, Jesus told the Jewish people that they would not see Him again until they said to Him, *"Blessed is He who comes in the name of the Lord."* Please pay close attention to the order of events here: the **"saying"** precedes the **"seeing."** You (the Jewish people) will not see me (Jesus) again until you say (to me): *"Blessed is He who comes in the name of the Lord."*

The simple truth about the second coming of Jesus Christ is that Jesus will not return **until** the Jewish people repent of their national unbelief and call for Him to come back from heaven. Although there has always been a remnant of Jewish believers, the Jews rejected Him as a nation, and they must call to Him as a nation to return. This dynamic should not surprise you. It is the final fulfillment of the pattern we see throughout the Book of Judges. The pattern is this: Israel is blessed but turns from the Lord to idolatry. Then God sends judgment and Israel is oppressed. In her oppression, she repents and calls out for God to send a deliverer, which He does (Judges 2:11-19, 3:9, 15, 4:3, 6:6-7).

Romans 11:15 reveals to us that when the Jewish people repent of their corporate and historical rejection of Jesus and receive Him as their Messiah, it will be *"life from the dead."* Many Godly scholars interpret this to be prophesying a great end time worldwide revival that includes the Jewish people (may this also happen!). I believe this is a reference to the resurrection of the dead that occurs when Jesus

CHAPTER 3 – SATAN'S MASTER PLAN TO PREVENT THE RETURN OF JESUS

physically returns (John 5:25-29; 1 Corinthians 15:51-53; 1 Thessalonians 4:14-17).

The prophet Zechariah saw God Himself pour upon all Israel the age ending supernatural revelation that Jesus is the Messiah. In Chapter 12 verse 10, he prophesied that God will *"pour out on the house of David and on the inhabitants of Jerusalem, the Spirit of grace and of supplication, so that they will look on Me whom they have pierced; and they will mourn for Him, as one mourns for an only son, and they will weep bitterly over Him like the bitter weeping over a firstborn."*

Zechariah also saw the Lord return. In Chapter 14 verses 3-4, he declared that *"The Lord will go forth and fight against those nations, as when He fights on a day of battle. In that day His feet will stand on the Mount of Olives, which is in front of Jerusalem on the east; and the Mount of Olives will be split in its middle from east to west by a very large valley, so that half of the mountain will move toward the north and the other half toward the south."*

(Please note that Zechariah saw Yahweh – God – standing on the Mount of Olives. This is another verse showing the deity of Jesus).

When Messiah Yeshua gloriously appears, He will raise the dead, destroy the wicked (1 Thessalonians 4:14-17; 2 Thessalonians 1:7; 2 Peter 3:7; Jude 1:15) and rule the nations from His throne in Jerusalem (Zechariah 12:10, 14:1-4; Matthew 23:39; Romans 11:15, 26).

The Jews receiving Jesus as their Messiah will be the final event that ushers in His return. This is why Satan has fought it so intensely and continues to do so. This highlights why anti-Semitism is such an insidious satanic strategy. The devil has set up an enormous smoke screen for the vast majority of Christians. Believers have often failed to follow the trail of clues given to us as we study both the Scriptures and history. These clues help us to pierce through the many layers of deception perpetrated by various anti-Semitic demonic doctrines. Christians have often failed to understand the profound prophetic importance of the Jewish people and the nation of Israel. The Jewish people are the central prophetic players in the end-time scenario that culminates in the return of their Messiah and King, Jesus.

While many Christians fail to see this connection, Satan knows it all too well, and he fights to keep it hidden in as many different ways as he can. So many Churches, ministers, and individual believers have different theological positions on the Jews and the nation of Israel. Consider your own beliefs about the Jewish people and the nation of Israel. What have you been taught? What do you think is the right attitude toward them? Are they just like any other people? Is Israel the same as any other nation? Or has God *chosen* the Jews for a particular purpose?

Current financial concerns, national and international political pressures, and various social and cultural issues all combine to influence the way many Christians relate to Israel and the Jewish people. Far too many Christians are more influenced by those dynamics than they are by the Scriptures. In the world today, these three areas - finances, politics, and culture – are all built upon unbiblical philosophies, values, and worldviews. They are the idols of our societies. We look to our money, our political leaders, and the latest cultural influences for our security and guidance instead of looking to the one true living God. When seen from this perspective, it is easy to understand how uninformed believers can unknowingly be used by Satan in his attempt to thwart the purposes of God.

As we watch the moral compass of our culture deteriorate and a parallel rejection of Biblical authority, we should not be surprised to see more and more anti-Semitic beliefs and practices emerge. These go hand in hand. The devil's attacks on the morality of a culture always bring with them a greater rejection of the God of Israel, His Holy Scriptures, the Jewish people and, since its establishment, the nation of Israel. The true Church also experiences greater rejection and persecution for her stand for God's purposes and Biblically based values. Don't be surprised if you experience these attacks. You are blessed when you do (Matthew 5:11; Luke 6:22; 1 Peter 3:14; 2 Peter 4:14).

When the Nazis first emerged as a political group, no one took them seriously. Hitler was demeaned and sneered at as a marginal ultra-right-wing rabble rouser. The lesson we must learn is that we have to pay attention to all the dynamics that are unfolding right before our eyes. Jesus repeatedly warned us to *"watch and pray"* (Matthew

CHAPTER 3 – SATAN'S MASTER PLAN TO PREVENT THE RETURN OF JESUS

24:42, 25:13, 26:41; Mark 14:38; Luke 21:36). We must be able to hear His voice in prayer so we can understand His will and our responsibilities in the days in which we live.

Zechariah 14:2 is clear that one of the hallmark events that immediately precedes the return of Jesus is the gathering of the nations which are seeking to destroy Jerusalem and Israel. Obviously, before this happens, there will be a massive international political movement that turns the entire world against Israel and the Jewish people. But it is God who is orchestrating this. As Zechariah 14:2 declares, God is *"drawing the nations to battle"* so He can defeat them.

As we *"search the Scriptures"* (John 5:39; Luke 24:27; Acts 17:11) we discover those things that God declared *"before they happen"* (John 13:19, 14:29). This gives us a solid Kingdom foundation and perspective so that we can become like the *"sons of Issachar"* who could accurately identify and interpret the *"signs of the times"* (1 Chronicles 12:32; Matthew 16:3; Luke 12:56). **It is crucial that we understand this because not every event is a prophetic sign.**

When authentic prophetic events do take place, we can identify them as *"that which the prophets have spoken"* (Acts 2:16). As we continually *"watch and pray"* (Matthew 26:41; Mark 14:38; Ephesians 6:18) we can hear what God is speaking to us. We must humbly seek to both give and receive Godly *"wisdom and counsel"* (Proverbs 15:22, 24:6) to confirm that we hear accurately. In this way, we will become *"wise as serpents"* (Matthew 10:16). We will not make *foolish decisions* based on disobedience, speculation or ignorance (Matthew 7:24-26; 2 Corinthians 2:11, 11:14; 2 Timothy 2:23). Because we *"examine, question and test everything"* (1 Thessalonians 5:20; 1 John 4:1), *"trusting the Holy Spirit to lead us"* (Psalm 143:10; John 16:13), and *"not depending on our ability to understand"* (Proverbs 3:5-6), we will *"make righteous assessments"* (John 7:24) and good balanced Godly decisions.

As we practice these things and mature in them *"our spiritual senses will become well trained"* (Hebrews 5:14) and we will grow in our ability to accurately discern the true nature of the present prophetic season and the spiritual battle we are engaged in (1 Peter 5:8; Ephesians 6:11).

We will not be *"shaken by every wave and wind of doctrine."* We will see through the *"tricks"* and *"deceitfulness"* of the *"ungodly motives"* of *"evil imposters," "hirelings"* and *"false prophets and teachers."* They are *"savage and ravenous wolves in sheep's clothing"* who even using *"lying signs and wonders," "deceive"* as they *"are being deceived."* Influenced by the *"activities of evil spirits"* they teach *"doctrines of demons"* (Matthew 7:15, 24:4-5, 11, 24; Mark 13:22; John 10:12; Acts 20:29; Ephesians 4:14; 1 Timothy 4:1; 2 Timothy 3:13; 2 Peter 2:1; Jude 1:4, 12, 13). Such evil people are motivated by only one thing, using YOU to fulfill their own ungodly and demonic goals (Romans 16:18; Philippians 3:19; 2 Peter 2:3, 19).

Only a spiritually mature international community of authentic disciples of the Lord Jesus will have the spiritual strength and discernment to resist the demonic pressures brought by the intense end time financial, political and cultural coercions and intimidations. Satan will use these as part of a final strategy to stop the true Body of Christ from being in proper Biblical relationship to the Jewish people. This is why it is so important for believers to understand that *the real spirit behind anti-Semitism is the spirit of anti-Christ.* Only when we understand what the spirit of anti-Semitism is and what it seeks to accomplish, can we rise up in "righteous indignation" and throw out any influence it has in our lives personally and in the Body of Christ at large.

Anti-Semitism is Supernatural and can be Subtle

Most people and far too many Christians, believe that anti-Semitism is merely a natural sociological, economic, cultural, religious or historical phenomenon. They have no idea about the real spiritual dynamics motivating it, or how subtly it can hide or disguise itself. It often manifests as an indifference and silence toward Jews and their enemies.

Far too many Christians do not understand that any time they allow themselves to harbor any anti-Semitic thoughts and feelings, they are

CHAPTER 3 – SATAN'S MASTER PLAN TO PREVENT THE RETURN OF JESUS

allowing the spirit of the Antichrist, who is seeking to prevent the return of Jesus, to influence their lives! When the Church acts, speaks, or even thinks in ways that are anti-Semitic or "Judeophobic," (i.e. a fear of Jewish people, Jewish things, or Judaism), she is aligning herself with her enemies and the enemies of the Lord Jesus Himself. *When the Church does not rise up in that "righteous indignation" against Israel's enemies and conduct herself with jealousy-provoking love, mercy, and power toward the Jewish people, she is working to prevent the return of her own Lord.* How many Christians would be shocked to read such a thing?

I am not talking about fleeting negative thoughts or feelings about a particular situation involving Jewish people, or about something the state of Israel does or fails to do. The spirit of anti-Semitism will look for opportunities to falsely accuse the Jewish people of things they are not guilty of. There are plenty of things the Jews, like all people, are guilty of, but we want to make sure we do not falsely accuse them, or anyone else for that matter. We need to follow the admonition of Jesus in John 7:24 and make a full investigation of all the facts before we come to any conclusion.

The problem arises when those thoughts and feelings develop into something much deeper and more pervasive in our souls. They open us up to the spirit of anti-Semitism that prevents us from loving and supporting the Jewish people as a testimony to them of what the Lord Jesus has done in our lives. Our hearts harden, and we fail to show them the mercy and forgiveness we have received from the Lord. The spirit of anti-Semitism, like all other demonic spirits of racial pride and prejudice, is a malicious, cruel spirit. Whenever and wherever it can get a foothold, it will eventually produce these three fruits of its demonic nature: hatred, persecution, and death. History is replete with horrific stories of the manifestations of that spirit in the lives of individuals, churches, and nations.

Does anti-Semitism, or Judeophobia, affect you? If so, have you ever considered that those negative thoughts and feelings about the Jews could be coming from demonic spirits? Test the spirits to expose their source (1 John 4:1). Ask the Lord to show you if anti-Semitic spiritual forces are influencing you and ask Him to shine the light of His Spirit upon your heart (Psalm 26:2, 51:7). If there is anti-Semitism there, repent and allow the Holy Spirit to root it out and replace it with the Father's thoughts and feelings for His beloved Israel (Isaiah 49:16).

All racial biases and prejudices are ungodly. We are called to love all people. It is the Spirit of God who puts the Love of God for all people into our hearts (Romans 5:5). This divine love is one of the primary fruits of the Holy Spirit in our lives. Anyone who says he is a "Christian" and does not have the love of God in his heart for all people is deceived about his spiritual condition (1 John 4:20). Christians who do not demonstrate love are spiritually immature (1 Corinthians 13). As you seek the Lord about His love for the Jewish people and His plans for them, you may be surprised at what He does in your heart. If you do not yet have the love of God in your heart for the Jewish people, you will! (Isaiah 49:15-16).

A word of caution is necessary here. Do not let your "end time theology" (eschatology) influence your heart attitude toward the Jewish people. Throughout the history of the Church, there have been many who only "loved" the Jews because they wanted to "convert" them. When the Jews did not respond as they desired, their hearts turned against them, and new waves of persecution erupted. This is what happened to Martin Luther. When the Jews did not respond to his "witness," he became their enemy. Because of experiences like this, Jewish people are very suspicious of Christians who say, "I love you." They will test your motives and your beliefs. Do not connect your love for the Jewish people or the nation of Israel with your end time theology. Love the Jewish people because God loves you and because you have His love in your heart for them. Show them the same mercy you have received (Romans 11:31). Just as God's love for you is unconditional, so your love for them must also be unconditional.

Since we all *"only know in part"* (1 Corinthians 13:9, 12), it follows that our understanding of the fulfillment of end time prophecies is also in part. Therefore, we must have a humble, teachable attitude about those prophecies, as well as our understanding of the prophetic meaning of present day events, particularly those concerning the Jewish people and the nation of Israel. When teaching about His second coming, Jesus Himself said that *"no one knows the day or the hour, except the Father alone"* (Matthew 24:36); therefore, we must readily admit that there is much we do not know. We must be very careful not to attempt to force our theology upon events that are unfolding almost every day. Let us follow the advice of the prophet Micah to *"...do justly, love mercy, and walk humbly with our God"* (Micah 6:8) and let the Father unfold His plan for the return of His Son as He will.

Please allow me to repeat and summarize. **When members of the Body of Christ fail to walk in love toward the Jewish people, they fail to provide them with a loving testimony of the Lord Jesus. When believers in Jesus fail to "testify" by their life, love, and power to the Jewish people of the reality of Jesus as the Messiah, they are hindering the return of the Lord!**

Jesus is waiting in Heaven for the Jewish people to call for Him to return. Those who rejected Him must receive Him. When they cry out to Him, *"Blessed is He who comes in the name of Lord,"* **Jesus will leave Heaven, raise the dead, return to Jerusalem, destroy the wicked and establish His reign over the entire earth!** (Matthew 23:39; Luke 13:35; Romans 11:12, 15; 1 Thessalonians 4:14-17; Zechariah 12:10, 14.4; Acts 1:11; Isaiah 2:3; Micah 4:2).

Amen! Come Lord Jesus!

CHAPTER 4 – FIGHTING THIS SPIRITUAL BATTLE

The battlefield of anti-Semitism will continue to increase as we move closer and closer to the return of the Lord. Satan's attacks on the Jewish people will intensify. The unrest in the Middle East will increase. The legitimacy of the State of Israel will continue to be undermined by various nations and political entities. For example, at the time of this writing the United Nations organization UNESCO issued a declaration that ignored any connection between the Jewish people and the Temple Mount and Western Wall worship site.

As you watch and pray, you will see both subtle and overt attacks on the Jewish people. As international unrest and economic uncertainty increases, the blame will be put on the Jews and Israel. Keep your eye on Iran and its threats to destroy Israel. Beware of the political power of oil producing nations. Watch what various Islamic terror groups are saying and doing to accomplish their goals. They are clear about announcing their intentions.

When they are defeated in one place, they will emerge in another. Their demonic inspiration will not rest. We must be equally diligent!

Do not be surprised if various so-called "Christian" leaders become more and more anti-Israel in their "theology." Satan has used those who called themselves "Christians" to persecute the Jewish people in the past. If he cannot instigate people to actual persecution, he will inspire theologies and belief systems that keep the Church either hostile to Israel and the Jewish people, or ignorant of God's purposes for them.

There are those "Christians" who seek to undermine the Jewish people's legitimate historic and Scriptural right to live in Israel. They advocate a theology that eradicates the purposes God has for the Jewish people and the Land of Israel. They replace it with the "Church" as "Spiritual Israel." They believe that there is no longer anything Biblical about the Jewish people as individuals, as a nation, or the actual land of Israel. It is as if they are all made to "spiritually disappear."

There are those who seek to delegitimize the Israeli government by accusing it of being an "Apartheid State" for building the security wall that has saved untold lives or calling for boycotts of Israeli products. If you want to boycott Israeli products, you will have to stop using most of your modern technology, as so much of it was created in Israel or by Jews (a quick search of the internet will show you this).

Study the history of the modern state of Israel, and you will see how many times the Israeli government offered peace deals to the so-called "Palestinians" (who didn't exist by that name until Yasser Arafat originated it) and were rejected because their leader's goal was to destroy Israel, not make peace. This continues to be their position.

This is not to ignore or minimize the many issues facing the so-called "Palestinian" people. But there are many ways to solve this problem if their leaders and the Arab nations had a genuine desire to do so. The first step would be to recognize Israel's right to exist as a Jewish state. The second would be renouncing the goal of Israel's destruction. Building upon these two foundation stones, the Arab world could use its massive amount of Petro-dollars to fund the creation of a new country, say in the northern part of the Sinai Peninsula.

It could also pay for the resettlement of those Palestinians who want to return to Jordan, the country that controlled the so-called "West Bank" before the six-day war. Others could return to Egypt which controlled the Gaza Strip. Of course, they could resettle in any other country, and money would be given to those countries also to fund this. The wealthy nations of the world, the World Bank, the International Monetary Fund and private billionaires could also invest in this history changing effort to create world peace.

Of course, this is all political fantasy and will never happen. But the point is if everyone really wanted peace, there are lots of ways and the means to create it.

Back to reality! If God is calling you to stand with His purposes for the Jewish people, you must have a strategy for fighting in this spiritual battle. You must know your place on this battlefield. Remember that spiritual warfare is always conducted from the place of victory

CHAPTER 4 – FIGHTING THIS SPIRITUAL BATTLE

already attained for us. We are battling an already defeated enemy. All we are doing in our battles is administrating, implementing, and achieving the victory the Lord Jesus won on the cross (Colossians 2:15). Ephesians 1:20-22 and 2:6 teaches us that *"we are now seated with Christ in Heavenly places far above all principalities and powers."* The throne of God is the place from which you conduct your spiritual warfare. You don't look at your enemy eye to eye; you look down upon him from your place of authority. We have *"authority over all principalities and powers"* (Luke 10:19). We have to learn how to exercise our authority and move ahead in obedience to the leading of the Lord.

This is not to minimize the battle or the reality of satanic abilities. The devil will fight against you in his attempts to discourage you and remove you from your place on the battlefield. As you choose to fight in this spiritual conflict, put on the *"armor of light"* (Romans 13:12; Ephesians 6:10-18). Use your various *"spiritual weapons"* (2 Corinthians 6:7, 10:4) and you will find that you have authority over every demonic power and plan. If you *"submit to God and resist the devil, he will flee from you"* (James 4:7). Will you choose to fight this spiritual battle?

A Prophetic Picture of this Warfare

In Exodus 17:8-16, God gives an extremely important prophetic understanding for waging war against the spirit of anti-Semitism. Here we see a clear picture of the enemy, the battle, and strategies for victory. Moses was leading the Israelites out of Egypt when they came into conflict with the Amalekites. This nomadic tribe that descended from Esau (Genesis 36:12) was attempting to destroy the people of Israel before they could enter into covenant with God on Mount Sinai (Exodus 19). This is yet another example of how Satan attempted to prevent God's purposes from being fulfilled.

Joshua led his army into battle with the Amalekites while Moses, along with Aaron and Hur, stationed themselves on a hill overlooking the fighting. As long as Moses kept his staff (the symbol of God's authority; see Exodus 4:17) over his head, Joshua's army was victorious. But as Moses' arms tired and the staff was lowered, the tide of the battle shifted, and Amalek gained the advantage. Moses then sat upon a stone while Aaron and Hur held up his arms, giving him the support he needed to keep the staff lifted up. The locale where the battle took place was called "Rephidim" or "Support" because Moses needed support to keep that symbol of God's authority lifted high over the battle, and that in turn supported the soldiers in combat.

It is very important to understand that at the victorious conclusion of the battle, Moses built an altar and named it *"Jehovah Nissi" – "The Lord is my Banner"* (Exodus 17:15). He understood that the staff he held up was a prophetic declaration, a Banner, or an Ensign in the spirit that brought the power of God to bear upon the battle and gave Israel the victory. This is one of the reasons we use banners, flags, staffs and other kinds of worship emblems in our praise, worship, and prophetic intercession. We wave our banners as prophetic proclamations that God will have the victory in the battles we face. His purposes will be established in our lives and in the lives of those for whom we intercede (Psalm 20:5, 60:4).

The staff Moses used was not only the prophetic symbol of his authority as God's representative, but it was also used to demonstrate God's power for the fulfillment of His purposes (Exodus 4:17). When the staff was lifted over the battle, God's authority was being exercised. The warriors could see it and knew they were fighting under its covering. We all need to understand the importance of acting under God's authority. Demons know when we are operating in that authority and when we are not (Acts 19:13-16). When God's Word and His Ways are not obeyed, when we desire something other than the fulfillment of His purposes, we come out from under that authority, and the demons will have an advantage over us (2 Corinthians 2:9-11).

However, whenever we repent and submit to His authority and seek the establishment of His Kingdom, the battle immediately turns and we are on the way to final victory (James 4:7). God in His wisdom has ordained this principle for spiritual warfare. He will not act on our behalf in battle if we are a disobedient army in disarray because we

CHAPTER 4 – FIGHTING THIS SPIRITUAL BATTLE

are seeking to build our own "empires of self." Nor will He give victory to those so-called leaders who misuse their spiritual authority, intimidating, manipulating, and controlling people for their own selfish ends. The abuse of spiritual authority is a serious crime in the Kingdom. It brings the severest of penalties (Luke 12:46; Matthew 24:51).

Aaron's and Hur's support kept the staff lifted up and assured that the Israelites would eventually defeat the Amalekites. Similarly, when we support each other in prayer, we are lifting up the Name of Jesus and the authority in that name, over and above all of the battles we face (Matthew 28:19; Luke 10:19; Ephesians 1:21; Colossians 2:10). Just as that ancient battle was fought until the sun set and victory was achieved, so we must have an attitude of perseverance, fighting without growing weary (Galatians 6:9), knowing that ultimately, we will have the victory.

When we are weary and feel like our spiritual strength and authority are weakening, we need those "Aarons and Hurs" the Lord sends us. We also need to serve others as they served Moses. Aaron and Hur did not say to Moses, "We will pray for you." They climbed the hill and stood there alongside him, holding up his arms. We also must do what the Lord commands in each battle we face. "Aarons and Hurs" bring powerful support in many different ways, not only by their intercession and prayers, but also by their words, financial support, and other acts of encouragement. This solid spiritual principle is seen throughout the Bible, and its enormous power has been testified to by the saints throughout history.

Exodus 17:16 tells us: *"The Lord will battle with Amalek from generation to generation."* This important Scripture reveals the true nature of our spiritual battle. It gives us important prophetic insight into the supernatural and generational nature of this conflict. Today we, as the army of God, are still fighting the same demonic powers the Israelites fought. Since this ancient battle continues in each generation, we see the spiritual dimension of this conflict. Ancient Amalek was defeated, yet the battle continues. The physical descendants of Amalek may not be engaged in battle against us, but the same spirits that motivated them to try to destroy the Jewish people are in operation today, still trying to prevent the purposes of God from being fulfilled. The same demonic powers that once sought to prevent Israel from coming into her inheritance in the land of Canaan are now trying to prevent both the Church and the Jewish people from preparing the way for Messiah's return.

The destinies of the Church and the Jewish people are intertwined. Satan knows this very well, so he works to keep them separated and, if possible, in mutual hostility. He works to hinder the Body of Christ from coming into unity and maturity, so that we will lack the ability to become the *"One New Man"* that beautifully demonstrates God's heart for the union of Jew and Gentile (Ephesians 2:14-16). Satan knows the authority the *"One New Man"* will have to provoke natural Israel to spiritual jealousy. He also knows very well what will happen when the Jews are provoked to jealousy. Their hearts will open to the revelation that Jesus is the Messiah. The prophecies of Zechariah will come to pass and the Jewish people will call for the Messiah to return to them and establish His Kingdom (Zechariah 12:10, 13:1; Matthew 23:39; Romans 11:12, 15).

In Exodus 17:14, God promised that He would *"utterly blot out the memory of Amalek from under Heaven."* In Numbers 24:20, there is a prophecy that declares when "Amalek" (who prophetically represents Satan) will finally be defeated and destroyed. This will happen when Messiah returns. The King James Version says, *"Amalek was the first of the nations,* (to try to destroy Israel), *but his end shall be destruction."* The Hebrew word translated *"his end"* is derived from the same root that we saw in Psalm 102:18 and can be translated "last days, end of the age, or final generation" (see how it is used in Isaiah 2:2; Daniel 10:14; Hosea 3:5; and Micah 4:1). So, we can accurately translate Numbers 24:20 to read, *"Amalek was the first of the nations, but he will be destroyed at the end of the age."* I believe we are at that time in history. Do you?

Is God calling you to be part of His end time army in this final battle that will end with the ultimate defeat of "Amalek?" Please prayerfully consider your answer to this question. It can change your life!!

CHAPTER 5 – UNDERSTANDING YOUR RELATIONSHIP TO HISTORY

To be successfully engaged in this spiritual conflict requires an understanding of the history of the Church and the Jewish people. It's crucial to read history books written from Jewish, Christian, and secular perspectives. This combination will hopefully give us a balanced view of each period that we study. Similarly, anyone involved in ministering to Muslims must read their history books and understand their perspectives.

In a moment of sheer and painful honesty, one Jewish woman once said to me, "Those Christians appear to be our friends, but just scratch below the surface, and you'll see; all they want to do is convert us or kill us." This statement brought home to me the present reality of the effects of the long and painful history of "Christian" anti-Semitism.

Built into the Jewish psyche is an emotional, psychological, and spiritual resistance to "Christianity" because of the "threat" they believe it poses to their survival as a people and as a religion. As one Rabbi said, "Would Christians be happy if there were no Synagogues left in the world?" We must understand the deeply rooted emotional, psychological, and spiritual realities of "Christian" anti-Semitism that has so deeply affected the Jewish people. This will help us develop patience and compassion as we relate to the Jewish people. For more on the history of "Christian" anti-Semitism, please read my book *So Deeply Scarred*.

Because God is the *"Alpha & Omega – the Beginning and the End"* (Revelation 21:6, 22:13), and can *"declare the end from the beginning"* (Isaiah 46:10), He does not see time or history as we do. He sees one continuous unfolding story. He sees our connection to the whole of the Church throughout history. He sees that for most of the history of the Church, the Jewish people have never heard the "true Gospel" of God's love, salvation, and redemption. What they did experience was the spewing forth of hatred and the perpetration of horrific crimes against them by a counterfeit "Church" in the Name of

Jesus. God sees the crimes of that "Church" and the pain it inflicted and the innocent blood it shed.

I want to share some things with you that I believe, and that I hope you will pray about before simply dismissing them. When the Lord began to lead me into these issues, He showed me that in the heart, mind, and spirit of the Jewish people there is a direct connection with their ancestors who suffered the horrific persecution of the "Church" in the Name of Jesus.

When the Jewish people have anything to do with "Christians" or "Christianity," it is as if on some deep primal level, they can "hear" the blood-curdling cries and heart-rending screams of those who suffered during almost 2,000 years of the most vicious kinds of hatred, persecution, and murder.

I don't want to seem overly dramatic. It is not a conscious hearing of actual screams, but something so deep and so profound, that there is often a physical response to the mention of the "Name of Jesus." Perhaps you have experienced that when you have tried to share your faith in Jesus with a Jewish person. You could feel a strong invisible barrier emerge, sometimes merely at the mention of His name. This wall is spiritual and comes from the horrific history the Jewish people have suffered in His name by His so-called followers.

Because of this long history of hatred, persecution, and death, the Jewish people, on that deep primal level, identify modern day "Christians" as the "spiritual descendants" of their persecutors. The Jewish people don't see you personally in that way. It is not rational to hold you responsible for something done in the past. I can only try to explain it as a spiritual phenomenon that is directly connecting them to their persecuted ancestors. They are responding to something in the deepest part of their being. It is not something that can be understood or explained in just natural ways.

It's as if the "blood-curdling screams of their ancestors" is built into their "spiritual DNA," and incorporated into the very fabric of their "Jewish identity" and "corporate consciousness." It rises up in a defiant resistance to the very thought of "converting" to the religion of

CHAPTER 5 – UNDERSTANDING YOUR RELATIONSHIP TO HISTORY

their enemies and to cease being Jews. This has helped me to understand why the Jewish people are so deeply antagonistic to the Gospel and belief in Jesus. It ironically is also part of the reason that the Jewish people today have a worldview that gives them permission to believe nothing, anything, or everything, and remain "Jewish," except that Jesus is the Messiah.

Of course, there is a demonic component to this. The devil uses the history of pain and suffering, and this inner response to that history of persecution, to exacerbate Jewish rejection of their own Messiah. But one day that will all change, and *"all Israel will be saved"* (Romans 11:26).

The "Christian" persecution of the Jewish people is a fact of history that will not change. Because of this history, I ask you to prayerfully also consider this: Is there is a "spiritual connection" between the Church of today and those who came before us claiming to represent Jesus? Has this "connection" created a "spiritual legacy" the Body of Christ inherited from those who identified themselves as "Christians" and persecuted the Jewish people in the Name of Jesus? I believe that the answer to these questions is Yes!

I believe that it is right to understand that we are their "spiritual descendants" because they went forth in the Name of Jesus, as we also do. If this is true, is there a supernatural demonic connection between their sins and crimes and us? Is the blood they shed somehow connected to us, as their "spiritual descendants?" Because of this connection, I believe that we are carrying a "guilt by association" with those "spiritual ancestors," even though we find the beliefs and behavior of those who persecuted the Jews in the Name of Jesus abhorrent, reprehensible and thoroughly anti-Christian.

While we recognize that we are not personally culpable for the sins of the past, we do have a responsibility to acknowledge them and become accountable for dealing with their present-day consequences. To dissociate ourselves from this sinful past, we must first recognize our association with it. This connection is built on the fact that those "Christians" claimed, as we do now, to represent our Lord and His Kingdom. Of course, we know that they did not. Once we recognize that association, we can reject and renounce it and move toward the goal of seeing the restoration of our relationship and responsibility to the Jewish people, and God willing, develop an effective ministry among the Jewish people and also on their behalf.

If this "connection" and "legacy" is true and real and we don't acknowledge it and reject it, does this open the door for the subtle activities of the demonic spirits of anti-Semitism to operate? I believe it does. Discarding this "connection" and "legacy" gives those demons a free course to operate, even in ways that are not overtly hostile to the Jewish people, but none the less, negatively impact both the Church and the Jewish people and undermine God's purposes for both groups.

For example, I believe that these demons are the source of the theology that some in the Church have embraced which teaches Christians to ignore, or reject, the Scriptural call to preach the Gospel to *"the Jew first"* (Romans 1:16). They replace that with the idea that "Jews have their own covenant and don't need Jesus," or "Jesus came for the Gentiles." Both of which are *"doctrines of demons"* that are completely contrary to the clear teachings of Scripture.

Another way these spirits continue to operate has nothing overtly to do with the Jewish people. They affect the way the Body of Christ relates to itself and the fulfillment of God's purposes. The demonic spirits that inspire anti-Semitic beliefs and practices work with spirits of anti-Christ. Together their nefarious influences and activities create the massive divisions and paralyzing disunity in the Body of Christ.

My heart quakes with fear as I write these words, but I am compelled to say them. The way most of the Church of the Lord Jesus relates to itself is treasonous. In my mind, treason, is the most serious crime you can commit against the King.

Jesus prayed that we would be *"one"* (John 17:11, 21–22), yet according to the Center for the Study of Global Christianity at Gordon-Conwell Theological Seminary, there are approximately 41,000

Christian denominations and organizations in the world (see: thoughtco.com/christianity-statistics-700533).

Until we recognize how the spirits of anti-Semitism and anti-Christ work, both independently and together, and how we have been, and continue to be influenced by them, the Body of Christ, as a whole, will continue to be divided, carnal, loveless, powerless, immature and ineffective.

If you don't think this is the condition of the Body of Christ, just look around at the conditions of countries and governments around the world. Look at how many unevangelized nations there are. Only a Spirit-empowered apostolic, prophetic and unified Church that knows how to "build itself up in love" and "share its resources" (Ephesians 4:11-16) will be able to fulfill her mandate to "evangelize and disciple every nation" (Matthew 24:14, 28:18-20; Colossians 1:28-29).

Could one of the sources of such "disunity" be directly connected to the horrific history of "Christian" anti-Semitism and the crimes the Church perpetrated against the Jewish people in the Name of Jesus? Could huge sections of the Church, which rejects that possibility, be opening the doors for the demonic activities and lies that continually create such massive distrust and division in the Body of Christ?

I believe that each of us must take personal responsibility to deeply and profoundly repent of everything that causes division in the Body of Christ, and ask the Lord how we can work to bring unity into His Church.

Please pray about this and see what the Lord shows you!!

If all of this is true, what can we do about it?

The only way to break any "connection" we might have with the demonic spirits of anti-Semitism and anti-Christ is by identifying and rejecting them, in the Name of Jesus. In this way, you begin to "take back" the illicit use of His name as the "authority" to persecute and kill Jewish people, as well as create divisions in the Body of Christ.

We can restore His Name to its proper place and usage as the "authority" to bring salvation, redemption, and unity (Acts 4:12, 10:43).

Then, both in intentional prayer and specific actions, declare your renunciation, rejection, and disassociation with the anti-Semitic demonic spirits that deceived and motivated the "Church" to perpetrate the crimes of persecuting and killing Jewish people. You can do the same thing with those demonic spirits of anti-Christ that create separation and division among the brethren (Proverbs 6:19).

As New Covenant priests (Romans 15:16; 1 Peter 2:5, 9; Revelation 1:6, 5:10), we can repent for the past (and present) sins of the Church. This is known as "Identificational Repentance," a form of repentance that is taught in the Scriptures. Nehemiah, Daniel, Isaiah and Ezra understood that they were repenting for the sins of their people and their ancestors ("we and our fathers"), so that a new time of reconciliation and healing could begin (Nehemiah 1:6, 9:2; Daniel 9:5, 15, 20; Isaiah 6:5; Ezra 9:6).

Such prayer and actions that renounce, reject, and disassociate ourselves from the "sins of the past" make a powerful declaration to the Jewish people and to the *"god of this world"* (2 Corinthians 4:4) that we want nothing to do with him or his evil works. We are renouncing his perversion of the Gospel and New Testament teaching about the Church and the Jewish people, particularly "replacement theology" and all of its evil fruit of hatred, persecution, and death. We are exposing those "demonic doctrines" for the lies they are, and we utterly and completely renounce and reject them.

In this way, in the spirit realm, you are putting yourself into the place where the Holy Spirit can begin to reveal to you God's plans and purposes for you in this battle against the demons of anti-Semitism. On a personal level, by intentionally breaking this connection, demons of anti-Semitism will no longer have any place of influence in your life, nor be able to taint your testimony to the Jewish people. When you take a stand in the spirit against those evil spirits, you also create a space for the Holy Spirit to impart to you, and through you, His love for the Jewish people and His strategies for sharing the Gospel with them. This is the love Jesus had in His heart when He *"wept over*

CHAPTER 5 – UNDERSTANDING YOUR RELATIONSHIP TO HISTORY

Jerusalem" (Luke 19:41), and the Apostle Paul carried as an *"unceasing burden for his kinsmen according to the flesh"* (Romans 9:3). You also may find your heart breaking as you see how Satan has used the "Church" to vilify the wonderful Name of Jesus for the Jewish people. Perhaps your tears will be the "seeds of intercession" the Lord will use to bring forth a great harvest of souls into the Kingdom of God!

When you break your connection to historic Christian anti-Semitism, and the Lord gives you an opportunity to share your faith in Jesus with a Jewish person, you might experience that person telling you that they "feel something different" about you. What's happening is that *they are not* feeling the presence of any anti-Semitic spirits (they are very sensitive to them – even if they don't recognize what they are feeling as demonic activity). What *they are* sensing in you is the presence of the Holy Spirit! Of course, they may not identify their "feeling" in this way. Experiences like this will encourage you to share the supernatural Love of God you have found in their Messiah! This is what the Church was always supposed to do; share the **Love of God**, not the **Hatred of the devil!**

It is also one of the reasons I wrote this book. I want to help bring healing to the historical wounds inflicted upon the Jews by the "Christian Church." As we understand this painful history, God can inspire us to bring His redemptive love to His covenant people.

There are many believers who desire to "apologize for the past" and declare their support for the Jews, and the nation of Israel, without understanding the entirety of their spiritual responsibility. God is seeking authentic disciples who will not only repent for the historical sins of the Church and lovingly support Jewish people and the nation of Israel, but who will also answer God's call to rise up in the power of the Holy Spirit to testify to them about what the Messiah did in their lives.

This is a witness that does not seek to "coerce" or "convert," but simply declares the reality of the Messiah in the lives of His true disciples. It is this testimony, coupled with overt acts of love and support coming from the international Body of Christ, that will be part of what I believe God will use to provoke natural Israel to spiritual jealousy

(Romans 11:11, 14).

Please understand that being a witness to the reality of the Messiah in your life does not mean that you have arrived at a place of "sinless perfection." The fact that you have been changed by Him, and are in the process of coming to spiritual maturity, is by itself a testimony to the work of the Holy Spirit in your life. If someone points the finger at your failings, just acknowledge them with grace and humility, thank the person who pointed them out, and continue to walk in love. Love is the single most important attribute of your spiritual life, and it is the most potent spiritual "weapon" you have (1 Corinthians 13:1-8). May we all be people who love freely and generously!

We must not be angry with the Jews for their resistance to the Gospel. After all, when most Jewish people hear anything about Jesus or Christianity, they immediately think that means betraying their people and converting to a Gentile religion which would make them a "non-Jew." Throughout their history, the Jewish people have been vilified for their "obstinate unbelief." But what exactly were they rejecting? What they witnessed in "Christianity" was a Torah rejecting, hate filled, persecuting Gentile religion. As if that wasn't enough, this religion's leaders had the audacity to demand that the Jewish people reject their own Torah and religious traditions, their own families, their own people, their own culture, and their own God! It is no wonder they remained in "obstinate unbelief." You would have also!!

Could it be that the Jewish people are a kind of spiritual "litmus test" for the Authentic Body of Christ? Could it be that Jewish unbelief is intended to provoke the "Body" to examine its life, faith, and practice? Could it be true that they are waiting for this authentic mature Church to arise and provoke them to faith?

Here are some other things for you to consider.

The vast majority of "Christendom," (i.e., all those who identify themselves with Jesus and the religion of "Christianity" in one form or another), is either ignorant of its historical and present-day sins against the Jewish people, or has ignored and refused to acknowledge and repent for them.

CHAPTER 5 – UNDERSTANDING YOUR RELATIONSHIP TO HISTORY

Has this given Satan "legal ground" in the spirit realm for *"doctrines of demons"* and *"activities of evil spirits"* (1 Timothy 4:1) to *"blind people's minds"* (2 Corinthians 4:4) to the truths of God's Word? Have these sins allowed a demonically inspired resistance to the flow of the gifts of the Holy Spirit? Is this one of the reasons (perhaps the major reason) the Church is so divided and experiences so little supernatural manifestation of the power of God?

These questions should provoke some serious thought, discussion, prayer, and study.

As we move closer and closer to the *"end of the age"* (Matthew 28:20), and sin comes to its full fruition (Matthew 13:39-40), Satan will do all he can to try to prevent the return of the Lord. We will see him rise up in fury against the Jewish people and the state of Israel. When this happens, will the Church stand with the Jewish people and the nation of Israel, or will the old anti-Semitic lies find new outlets in the Church? How eternally ironic would it be if the Church becomes one of Satan's unwitting accomplices in preventing the return of her own Lord, by assisting in or merely allowing the Jews, or Israel, to be destroyed.

It is not hard to imagine Church leaders from around the world justifying the death of the state of Israel and the final extermination of the Jewish people. The replacement theologians will have a field day proclaiming things like, "We told you God was finished with the Jews. We are the real spiritual 'Israel,' not the 'political Zionist state.' It is better for world peace to finally be through with the Jews." (Oh, by the way, those who believe that and welcome the Muslims, will be utterly shocked when the Muslims turn against them, and "force" them to convert to Islam).

Allow me to propose something else to consider: Could it be that many "Christians" have been deceived into practicing aberrant forms of the "religion of Christianity" instead of being authentic disciples of the Kingdom of God? This is the religion that typically creates mere "Churchgoers." These are people with little or no faith, love, supernatural power, or fruit of the Spirit, and so sadly, no desire for them. This is a religion that often puts a superficial "veneer" of "Christian" vocabulary, theology, and rituals upon an essentially natural worldly existence that bears no fruit for the Kingdom of God. This is also the religion that has a "legacy of hatred" and "theologies of contempt" for the Jewish people.

If the Jews are a "litmus test" and God intends to use authentic disciples to bring them to their Messiah, we must cooperate with the Holy Spirit as He works to deliver the Body of Christ from the many aberrancies of "Christianity" and bring her to maturity (Ephesians 5:27). In balance with this, we must understand that it is also true that sometimes even seeing the "real thing" will not necessarily bring anyone to faith. History and the Bible itself are replete with examples of this. Coming to faith in Jesus is the sovereign, supernatural work of God Himself. Jesus said that *"no one can come to Me unless the Father draws him"* (John 6:44, 65). Only God can reveal that Jesus is the Messiah (Matthew 16:17). But the Biblical truth remains that God's plan is to use His people as His witnesses (Isaiah 43:10; Acts 1:8), and we are called to be the most authentic witnesses that we can be (Matthew 5:14-16; Philippians 2:15).

Some time ago I was told this story. A large Christian college sponsored an event to show their support for the state of Israel and the local Jewish community. A prominent Jewish leader stood at the podium and said only three words to the Christian audience: "Make me jealous," and then sat down. In other words, "If you have the real thing, prove it to me."

I also heard about a Synagogue that was badly burned by a group of neo-Nazi skinheads. The local Christian community was outraged by this and came together to help the Jewish congregation rebuild. Hundreds of believers donated time, money and supplies. As they were working alongside the members of the Synagogue, one of the Jewish leaders said to one of the pastors, "You are taking away my reason for not believing." The love this Jewish leader was receiving was showing him the "real thing."

As I was speaking at a conference on the "Jewish Roots of Christian faith," I had a moment of insight and understanding into this. I believe

CHAPTER 5 – UNDERSTANDING YOUR RELATIONSHIP TO HISTORY

the Lord showed me that the Jewish people today are waiting to see the manifestation of the authentic Body of Messiah. In that brief moment, I could see that the Jewish people want to know if Jesus is truly their Messiah. But because of the sins of the "historic Christian religion" and the lack of love, unity, and power in the "Church" today, they have not been able to believe. It is not a matter of what the Rabbis taught or what their traditional beliefs are. These are not the important factors for them.

The real issues are:
- The pain of past persecutions they still feel.
- The threat to their identity and survival as Jews that Christianity has historically presented to them.
- The lack of supernatural reality they observe in the "Christian religion."

I believe the Lord showed me that what they are secretly waiting for, as proof that Jesus really is the Messiah (although they would probably never admit it if you asked directly), is a true demonstration and manifestation of the Kingdom of God (1 Corinthians 2:4-5, 4:20).

Are the Jewish people watching for, and waiting for, the authentic Body of Christ to provoke them to jealousy? I believe they are! This is one of the great challenges before the Church today.

As you understand the history of the Church and the Jewish people and recognize what the Lord is assigning you to do, you will discover God's grace and favor in amazing ways. As you say "yes" to the Lord, He will enable you to see the battlefield and your responsibilities in the battle. We must all face the reality of the battles objectively so that we can respond properly. We must be like Joshua and Caleb, who like the other ten spies recognized that they were facing great enemies, but rejected their fear and unbelief. They chose to believe that God would keep His word and give them victory (Numbers 13:25-14:9). Always remember this, *"The battle belongs to the Lord"* and *"unless He builds the house, we labor in vain"* (1 Samuel 17:47; Psalm 127:1). Because ultimate victory is guaranteed (1 Corinthians 15:57; 2 Corinthians 2:14), let us *"press on to the goal"* (Philippians 3:12-14). We have read the end of the Bible, and we win!

What if...?

We recognize that Jewish people see history through the lens of all they suffered. They see "Christian" anti-Semitism and its "theology of contempt" as the real source of the Holocaust. But what would history look like if the Church had instead developed a "Love the Jews" theology? What would history look like if Church leaders – men like Chrysostom and Luther – had understood that it is the demonstration of love and power that would provoke natural Israel to spiritual jealousy? For one thing, it would have inspired them to raise up spiritually mature disciples filled with the love of God and the power of the Holy Spirit. (Shouldn't this be the testimony of the Body of Christ today?).

If the Church had developed a "Love the Jews" theology, I truly believe that the beautiful power of love would have overcome the resistance of Jewish people to the Gospel. The witness of authentic disciples would have (and still can!) raised many profound and searching questions like, "Who is this Jesus these Gentiles talk about? They claim He is alive from the dead and is doing miracles in their lives. They say it is His Spirit that is inspiring them to love us. Could it be that He is our Messiah?"

It is very hard to resist a message of love brought by truly loving people. The history of the world would have been very different if the Church had obeyed the revelation she originally received to make, mature, and send disciples filled with love and power.

The future of the world can be molded by such a Church. We face many great challenges, but hearts and lives filled with the Love and Power of God can overcome them. We can bring millions of souls into the Kingdom of God and, I pray and believe, provoke natural Israel to spiritual jealousy.

CHAPTER 6 – DOCTRINES OF DEMONS VS. BIBLICAL TRUTHS

As we study the history of the Church and the Jewish people, we will see the Church's *"arrogance toward the branches."* After being *"cut off from the root of the Olive Tree,"* (Romans 11: 18-22), the Church was deceived into rejecting, hating, and persecuting the Jews.

Satan, the great deceiver, who is the *"Father of lies"* (John 8:44; 1 John 5:19; Revelation 12:9), convinced the Church leaders that his *"demonic doctrines"* were the truth. In so doing, he perverted the minds of those leaders and their followers to such a degree that they believed they had a divine mandate and theological justification for oppressing and killing Jewish people.

The Devil's influence was (and is) so powerful that he completely wiped away normal human moral sensibilities, thoroughly twisted or erased the commands of the Scriptures, and thereby allowed his demons to powerfully manipulate the Church. The effect of these lies cannot be overestimated or overstated.

All this hatred and persecution only intensified the Jewish rejection of Jesus and increased the hardness of their hearts against Him.

As a small way of introducing some of this history, read the following five notorious demonically inspired lies that have done immense damage to the Jewish people and the Church.

Lie # 1 - The Jewish people "killed Christ" and therefore all Jews of every generation are guilty of the crime of deicide (killing God).

The truth is:
No one "killed Christ." Jesus went to the cross voluntarily. He said, *"For this reason the Father loves me, because I lay down my life so that I may take it again. No one has taken it away from me, but I lay*

it down on my own initiative. I have authority to lay it down, and I have authority to take it up again. This commandment I received from My Father" (John 10:17-18).

The truth is:
Jesus died according to the predetermined plan of God (Acts 2:23; 1 Peter 1:20; Revelation 13:8). God sacrificed His son on our behalf to make atonement for our sins. God the Father was directly responsible for the death of Jesus (Isaiah 53; 1 Corinthians 15:3). On the Cross, Jesus declared forgiveness to those who betrayed and executed Him (Luke 23:34). He did not call for revenge.

The truth is:
The Romans crucified Jesus. Crucifixion was a Roman, not a Jewish, form of execution. We have never heard Christians call for the persecution of the Romans or their descendants, the Italians. We have never heard the cry, "Kill the Italians, they killed Christ!" Of course not, because Satan is no more interested in killing those people than he is in killing anyone else. He is, however, very interested in killing Jews because their prophetic destiny is tied to the return of the Messiah and his destruction.

The truth is:
Our sins crucified Jesus. He died for all of us willingly, because that was how God intended to make atonement for the sins of all humanity (Romans 5:6-11; 1 Corinthians 15:3; Matthew 26:26-28).

It is true that a small group of Jewish leaders and their immediate followers participated in the political maneuvering and conspiracy with the Romans that led to the execution of Jesus. They arranged for His betrayal and arrest; they illegally tried Him, and they turned Him over to the Romans for execution (Acts 2:23, 3:14-18). They were part of the divine plan, but will still answer for their actions.

All the Jewish people and leaders alive at that time were not part of this plot, did not even know about it, and were certainly not guilty of killing Jesus. Many thousands of Jews became believers after the day of Pentecost (Acts 2:41, 4:4, 21:20).

Satan has successfully used this lie to manipulate the Church into persecuting Jews as a punishment for this crime. This has also had the secondary effect of so completely alienating the Jewish people from their own Messiah, that they have been effectively prevented from coming to faith in Jesus. Simply stated, lie #1 manipulated the Church to persecute the Jews in the Name of Jesus and prevent the Jews from coming to faith in Him. God's desire for His Church has always been, and remains, to lovingly inspire the Jewish people to faith in their Messiah. The contrast between the two motives reveals the spirit behind each.

Lie # 2 - God rejected and abandoned the Jewish people as their punishment for the crime of killing Jesus.

The truth is:
God has never rejected the Jewish people. *"I say then, God has not rejected His people, has He? No, certainly not!"* (Romans 11:1).

> *"Thus says the Lord, who gives the sun for light by day and the fixed order of the moon and the stars for light by night, who stirs up the sea so that its waves roar; The Lord of Hosts is His name: If this fixed order departs from before Me, declares the Lord, "Then the offspring of Israel also will cease from being a nation before Me forever."* (Jeremiah 31:35-36)

Lie # 3 - The Church replaced the rejected Jews and became the "new" or "spiritual" Israel.

The truth is:
The Church never became a "new" or "spiritual" Israel in replacement of natural Israel. By receiving the Jewish Messiah, Gentile believers were *"grafted into Israel's Olive Tree"* and became part of the *"Commonwealth of Israel"* (Ephesians 2:12-19; Romans 11). God never made a covenant with the Church. He made a New Covenant with Israel and opened that covenant to the nations of the world (Isaiah

49:6; Jeremiah 31:31; John 10:16; Acts 10). In this way, the Body of Messiah is joined to natural Israel. Gentile Christians do not replace Jews; they are grafted into and joined with the Jewish people. (Romans 11: 17-24).

Lie # 4 – The Church must persecute the Jewish people as a punishment for their crime of deicide.

The truth is:
Because of this "grafted-in" relationship, the Church was called to show mercy to Israel, provoke them to spiritual jealousy (Romans 11:11, 31), and inspire faith in Jesus, not persecute them and drive them away from that faith.

Imagine two people standing next to each other with one arm around each other's waist. One person represents the Church, the other the Jewish people. Linked together with heads turned toward each other they are joined in a face-to-face relationship. This is God's prophetic picture of the relationship that should exist between the Church and the Jewish people. The picture Satan has worked to produce is very different. Now imagine the person who represents the Church removing their arm from the waist of the other person, turning him away and then repeatedly stabbing him in the back. This picture illustrates the historic satanically inspired rejection of the Jewish people and the ensuing adversarial and hostile relationship between the Church and the Jewish people.

Which picture are you a part of? Are you standing in a connected face-to-face "grafted-in" relationship with the Jewish people as Romans 11:17-24 teaches? If not, why not? Even if you would never consider yourself an anti-Semite or someone who would ever stab the Jewish people in the back, are you just on the sidelines merely watching others get involved in God's plans? By sitting passively, watching the events of our times and not being actively involved, you are indirectly helping Satan's plans. Remember the words of the great statesman Edmund Burke, *"All that is necessary for the triumph of evil is that good men do nothing."* Open your heart to God's plans for the restoration of the Church to her Biblical relationship and responsibility to

CHAPTER 6 – DOCTRINES OF DEMONS VS. BIBLICAL TRUTHS

the Jewish people. Ask Him what you are supposed to do.

Lie # 5 - This "punishment" of the Jews serves as a warning to all people who reject Christ.

The truth is:
The Jewish people were not exiled and then persecuted as a warning to those who reject Christ. That is another doctrine of demons that ignorant and arrogant people use to justify their evil acts.

God warned the Jewish people that the consequences of their rebellion and disobedience to Him and His Torah would be expulsion from the land of Israel, exile among the nations and great suffering (Leviticus 26 and Deuteronomy 28). Israel has a long and tragic history of disobeying God and rejecting the prophets sent to warn them of impending judgment. This disobedience culminated in the rejection of their Messiah. In Luke 19:41-44, Jesus, while weeping, told the Jewish people that they would undergo horrific suffering because they *"did not recognize the time of their visitation"* (Luke 19:44). Even though they rejected their Messiah, God did not reject them! (Romans 11:1). He never will! (Jeremiah 31:35-37).

Doctrines of Demons

Other lies and demonic doctrines infected the Church with the intention of keeping Christians in an adversarial, hostile, and persecutory relationship with the Jewish people. Major examples of these were:

1) The notorious **"Blood Libel."** In this perfidious lie, Jews were accused of killing a Christian child and using its blood to prepare the Passover meal. Preached in Churches during the Passover season, this insidious doctrine was the catalyst for many anti-Jewish riots and massacres.

2) Jews were accused of being responsible for the **Black Plague** by **poisoning wells**. Because of Jewish religious hygienic practices and because Jews typically lived in segregated areas with

their own wells, there was less infection in the Jewish community. This caused speculation that the Jews had started the plague by poisoning "Christian" wells. By the way, it was the Catholic Pope Gregory IX who, believing that cats were demonic creatures, ordered their extermination in Europe in 1232. This led to the population explosion of rats – who were the carriers of infected fleas – that caused the plague.

3) Another popular and particularly weird accusation, was the **"Host Desecration"** slander. Jews were accused of stealing the "Host" (the wafer used in the Catholic mass) and stabbing it repeatedly because they hated Jesus so much that they wanted to continue killing Him. This was also used as a catalyst for persecution and murder of the Jewish people.

Church leaders also believed that the Jewish rejection of Jesus as the Messiah could be perceived by potential converts as a threat to the veracity of the Christian religion. Vying for converts in the Greco-Roman world, the Jews proclaimed that they were the much older, and therefore more authentic, religion. This gave them additional credence with the pagans who valued the fact that Judaism had an ancient history. To undermine this supposed position of superiority, the Church leaders went to extreme lengths to undermine the Jewish religion which also opened the way for the persecution of the Jews.

The Jewish rejection of Jesus is one of the main points that establishes His Messiahship. It proved the veracity of the Scriptures which taught that the Jewish people would indeed reject their own Messiah (Isaiah 49:7, 53:3; Psalm 118:22) and that He would become a *"light to the Gentiles"* (Isaiah 42:6, 49:6). Instead of vilifying the Jewish people, Church leaders should have been working to make and mature true disciples who would grow in love and power and provoke the Jews to spiritual jealousy.

Having been infected by these and other detestable doctrines, Christianity continued its long and painful history of hating, persecuting and killing Jews. Instead of being what God intended, a Spirit-filled community demonstrating the reality of the Kingdom of God, the Church came under satanic influence, was filled with hatred, and committed murder. The plain facts of history give us clear proof of that. Satan is the hate-filled murderer (John 8:44), and the false leaders who promulgated those heinous doctrines were influenced by his lies and his demonic underlings (2 Corinthians 11:14; 2 Peter 2:1; 1 Timothy 4:1). Jesus said that *"we can know a tree by its fruit"* (Matthew 12:23). The fruit of these "ministers" was hatred, persecution, and death. They said they represented Jesus, but the evil fruit they bore revealed the satanic spiritual source that inspired them.

But thank God, we are now living in a time when God is restoring the authentic Body of Christ to her Biblical relationship and responsibility to the Jewish people. Christians around the world, are coming to grips with the Church's anti-Semitic past and repenting of it. Ministries and individual believers from many nations are working with, and for, the Jewish people politically, practically, and spiritually. For example, many ministries are reaching out to help Jews immigrate to Israel and build new lives there.

Each of these outreaches is an authentic demonstration of the Kingdom of God. Inspired by the Holy Spirit, they do not go unnoticed by the Jewish people. While leading a tour to Israel, I heard first-hand testimonies of the positive effect it has when believers who visit Israel proclaim their love for the Jewish people and the God of Israel. God uses these expressions of love and support to heal the hurts of history and eradicate the stigma of anti-Semitism that the Jewish people have historically attached to "Christianity."

CHAPTER 7 – SHARING YOUR FAITH WITH THE JEWISH PEOPLE

The Importance and Power of Unconditional Love and Evangelism

Healing the ancient wounds of anti-Semitism can be accomplished by demonstrations of unconditional love and support for the Jewish people around the world. This love must not be tainted by any expectations that the Jewish people will come to faith in Jesus, or even act or speak in ways that please us. As believers, we are simply called to be witnesses. We must understand that no one comes to believe in Jesus apart from a direct personal revelation from God Himself (John 6:44, 65; Matthew 16:17).

For centuries, the Church ignored this simple Biblical truth and forced Jewish people to "convert to Christianity" in the most horrific ways. People can be forced into changing all manner of external behavior, so they appear to say and do what is expected. No one is ever coerced into changing what they believe or becoming a true disciple of the Lord Jesus. This is why emotionally manipulative evangelistic techniques practiced in some Churches never work. All such practices are opposite to the teachings of the Bible and contrary to the ways of the Lord. Everyone has to freely choose to open their heart to receive the Lord Jesus. God does not 'force' Himself upon anyone. He invites us into a personal love based relationship with Himself (John 1:11-13; Revelation 3:12). It is *"the goodness of God that leads people to repentance"* (Romans: 2:4). The evil of men drives people away from God.

God looks at the heart, but the heart did not matter to the corrupt leaders of the Church. Obedience to their authority is all that concerned them. It has been said that bad theology is a cruel taskmaster. History has proved the veracity of this statement as these corrupted leaders created perverted theologies that justified their persecution of the Jewish people and all others who stood in their way.

The fact that many of these persecutors truly believed their actions were "righteous and Godly" is evidence of Satan's ability to deceive (John 8:44; 2 Corinthians 11:3; Revelation 12:9). Nazi perpetrators of the Holocaust, and those who collaborated with them, thought that by ridding humanity of the Jews (and other "inferior" people), they were making the world a better place. In Hitler's infamous manifesto *Mein Kampf* (My Struggle), he wrote: "I believe that I am acting in accordance with the will of the Almighty Creator: by defending myself against the Jew, I am fighting for the work of the Lord."

If the leaders of the Church down through the centuries truly loved God and believed the Bible, they would have known that love is the most important expression of the Kingdom of God (1 Corinthians 13). They would have taught their people to love God, their neighbors, and even their enemies (Deuteronomy 6:5; Luke 10:27; Matthew 5:44). Even if they believed the Jews were their "enemies" because of their resistance to the Gospel, they were commanded by their Jewish Lord to love them!

Thousands of times, the Jews were forced to "convert" upon pain of death, or loss of children, or oppressive taxation, or expulsion, or other forms of persecution. This was not "conversion" in any Biblical sense of the word. It was "external submission" to a religious/political "institution." This "institution" was an abhorrent aberrancy that masqueraded as the authentic Church. It did not represent the Kingdom of God! It was a counterfeit of the genuine Body of Christ!

Because of the history of "forced conversions," most Jewish people have a deep disdain for the word "conversion." But "conversion" is not a "dirty" word. It reflects the Hebrew word "Shuv" which means "to turn" or "to repent" and is one of the most beautiful concepts in the entire Bible (Psalm 51:13). God invites everyone to "turn" toward Him. Our "turning" toward Him is the beginning of repentance, and gives all who do an opportunity to be forgiven and receive new life from the Lord. Simply put, it means we get "another chance." If we understand "conversion" in this way, as an offer to receive new life, we see that "conversion" is one of the most wonderful, magnificent words in any language.

CHAPTER 7 – SHARING YOUR FAITH WITH THE JEWISH PEOPLE

When Jewish people come to personal faith in Yeshua the Messiah ("Jesus Christ"), they are not "converting" to a Gentile religion called "Christianity." They experience a supernatural life-changing encounter with the Living God. They are spiritually *"born from above"* (John 3:3-8; 1 Peter 1:3, 23) and experience a supernatural *"regeneration and renewing by the Holy Spirit"* (Titus 3:5). They are *"grafted back into their own natural Olive Tree"* (Romans 11:23-24). Their personal relationship with the God of their Fathers, the God of Abraham, Isaac, and Jacob, the God of Israel, is restored. They experience a supernatural *"transfer from the kingdom of darkness into the Kingdom of God's beloved Son"* (Colossians 1:13).

This is authentic "Biblical Conversion." It is a "turning," a "conversion," from sin to salvation, from darkness to light, from death to life! It has been experienced by myriads of people from every nationality down through the ages who have testified to the supernatural reality of this "conversion,"

This experience is not limited to one's initial encounter with God but is an important ongoing part of our spiritual lives. We can live a lifestyle of repentance and continually receive His gracious loving mercy, forgiveness and new life (Proverbs 24:16; James 4:10; 1 Peter 5:6).

God never made a covenant with the Church or with any nation other than Israel. What He did was offer the nations of the world an opportunity to enter His "New Covenant" with the Jewish people (Jeremiah 31:31; Luke 22:20). All authentic Christians are practicing a "Jewish" religion. Everything about Biblical "Christianity" is Jewish. Before the New Testament was written and canonized, the only Bible of the early Church was the Hebrew Scriptures. Christians believe in the Jewish Messiah and worship the God of Israel. They receive the New Covenant Scriptures as authoritative, written by or under the auspices of Jewish Apostles.

All of the doctrines and practices of Biblical Christian faith are rooted in the Hebrew Scriptures. Justification by faith in Messiah's sacrificial blood atonement, personal sanctification, water baptism, communion, public worship, preaching and teaching, Bible studies, laying on of hands, anointing with oil, prayer, fasting, intercession and fellowship (with food!) are all expressions of the *"rich root of the Olive Tree"* (Romans 11:17).

In fact, all Gentiles who authentically believe in the Jewish Messiah, (some say they are "converted to Christianity") are really "converted" to what can be called "New Covenant Messianic Judaism." They can even consider themselves to be "spiritually Jewish" (Romans 2:29) because their faith in Jesus/Yeshua the Messiah spiritually connects them to the Jewish people and the God of Israel. By faith in Jesus/Yeshua, they are *"grafted into Israel's Olive Tree"* (Romans 11:17), are *"made fellow citizens with the saints,"* and are part of the *"Commonwealth of Israel"* (Ephesians 2:12, 13, 19). All of this is only made possible through this *Jewish New Covenant* (Romans 11:25; Jeremiah 31:31-34).

It is important to emphasize that Gentile believers do **not** become "Jews," nor should they consider themselves "Jewish." Gentiles who come to faith in Yeshua the Messiah do not change their natural ethnicity. A Chinese person who comes to faith in the Jewish Messiah is still Chinese. Their ethnicity does not change; their spiritual identity does!

Beware of Hidden Agendas

If God has given you a desire to share your faith in Jesus with Jewish people and you are praying earnestly for them to have a revelation that Jesus is their Messiah, you must never let your witness be tainted by any "hidden agendas."

We must not let our zeal to share the Gospel overshadow our love for those with whom we share it. Zeal must be tempered by wisdom, and then empowered by love. *"We love because He first loved us"* (1 John 4:19) and we love because He imparts His love to us (Romans 5:8; Ephesians 2:4-5; 2 Corinthians 5:14). We must love unconditionally, without expecting anything in return (1 Corinthians 13:4-8), and because we often fall prey to human weaknesses, we must be diligent to keep our love pure and undefiled (Jude 1:21).

CHAPTER 7 – SHARING YOUR FAITH WITH THE JEWISH PEOPLE

Because of their corporate history and personal experiences, most Jewish people suspect ulterior motives in people who identify themselves as "Christians." They will be watching to see if the only reason you are relating to them is to "convert" them. You can expect Jewish people to be wary of your motives. They will test your love to see if their apprehensions are justified. This is understandable and it is also okay. It gives you an opportunity to demonstrate the authenticity of your love. Hidden agendas develop when we have impure motives.

If there are ulterior motives, then our so-called "Christian love" will turn cold when hidden agendas are thwarted. Superficial love will turn to bitterness, resentment, anger, and hatred when those whom you "love" do not respond as you want them to. When Jews see this behavior in Christians, they understand that "love" was nothing more than a desire to "convert" them. We have personally observed this with people who are involved in cults. They only showed affection to us when we were considered potential converts. When they realized that we were not going to join them, they no longer wanted a relationship with us. They proved that they did not love us. Their real agenda was to get us to join their cult.

As I wrote earlier, a powerful and historically devastating example of hidden agendas is seen in the life of Martin Luther. Early in his ministry, he looked with favor upon the Jews, but only with a motive to "convert" them. When the Jews rejected his witness, he turned against them with a hateful vengeance, writing his infamous little book *"On the Jews and Their Lies."* Though small, it profoundly influenced the Lutheran church and became a major source for the "legacy of hatred" that eventually culminated in the Holocaust. During the Nuremberg trials for war crimes, high-ranking Nazi leaders cited their Lutheran traditions as part of the religious justification for their evil.

Unconditional love is a very powerful witness of your faith. Love will open appropriate opportunities for you to share your testimony and faith in Jesus. Therefore, rest in the Lord, and leave the results in God's hands. It is the Holy Spirit's job to bring revelation to those whom the Father is calling (John 6:44, 65). We have great rest and peace when we understand that we cannot do the Holy Spirit's job. We have not been called, or anointed, to be "soul-winners." The Holy

Spirit is the "soul-winner." He is the one who brings conviction, revelation, and understanding (John 14:26, 16:8; Ephesians 1:17). We have no such abilities. But we have been called and anointed to be witnesses (Acts 1:8). Learn how to "rest" in the Lord, doing what you can, when you can, with those you can. Then trust the Lord without any sense of guilt, ("I haven't done enough") or condemnation ("If only I ...."), and watch God work as you pray for those to whom you witness, Jew or Gentile.

Let your love be **pure**, let the Holy Spirit lead you and do what only He can do. God will give you the opportunities to share your faith in the Messiah. Your love will provoke questions and the Holy Spirit will give you wisdom in how to respond (Luke 12:12; Proverbs 11:30).

Remember, love is patient (1 Corinthians 13:4), so you must be patient and prayerful, trusting the Holy Spirit to bear witness of Jesus to the Jewish people. If they reject Him or your testimony of Him, don't be discouraged. Keep on loving, keep on praying, because you never know what the Lord will do in response to your prayers. When God wanted to knock Rabbi Saul of Tarsus off his "high horse" (or camel!) and reveal Jesus to him, He knew how to do it (Acts 9:1-19).

As you keep your heart in the Love of God (1 Peter 1:22), typical Jewish resistance to the Gospel will not frustrate you. You will not be put off by condescending looks and patronizing comments that may accompany a Jewish person's response to an "ignorant or ill-informed" Gentile talking about their "faith in Jesus." Their resistance is not your responsibility. You do not even have to address it. Your responsibility is to ask the Lord how He would have you respond, not react. If you are unsure of how He would have you respond, remember the right response is always founded upon love and will express that love and the other fruits of the Holy Spirit (Galatians 5:21-22).

The more you learn about Jewish history and beliefs, the more you will understand this resistance. You will be able to continue to walk with your Jewish friends, not with a "hidden agenda" to see them "convert to Christianity," but with a sincere motivation for God to reveal Jesus to them as you continue to be an example of His love and

CHAPTER 7 – SHARING YOUR FAITH WITH THE JEWISH PEOPLE

power. When it is appropriate, it is certainly proper to tell your Jewish friends that you are praying for that revelation to happen. As you keep your heart in the love of God, you will be able to pray for them effectively. Stand back and watch what God will do in answer to such prayers. Our lives, our love, and our testimony are vehicles that the Lord can use to stimulate their hearts and minds. When all is said and done, only a supernatural revelation can bring them to faith in Jesus. You are not the one who gives revelation; it is the work of God Himself (Matthew 16:17; Luke 10:22; John 6:44; 1 Corinthians 2:10). Remember, He is the "soul winner," not you!

When your love is tested, and your motives are examined or even challenged, you can rest in the knowledge that your desire for the Jewish person to come to faith in Jesus did not come from you, it will not be completed by you, and it is not your responsibility. Your responsibility is to love, share the reason for that love when appropriate, and leave everything else to the Lord. Remember the words of Psalm 127:1, *"Unless the Lord builds the house, they labor in vain who build it."*

One of the most important and most exciting parts of standing against anti-Semitism is the opportunity we have to see God pour out His revelation of Jesus upon the Jewish people (Zechariah 12:10, 13:1; Matthew 16:17; John 1:13). We do not have to try to do anything in the flesh, like compelling them to "make a decision for Christ." Believe me, when Jewish people make up their minds to do something or believe something, no one is going to dissuade them. They typically will make a wholehearted commitment to follow what they believe is right. We see evidence of this historically in Jewish involvement in various political causes and social justice issues, such as the American Civil Rights movement and the socialist/communist revolutions of the early twentieth century. We also see this demonstrated in the fact that when a Jewish person comes to faith in Jesus as their Messiah, they are usually very zealous for the Lord.

One of Satan's tactics will be to try to make you feel ashamed of your faith, or the Gospel, or the Church, or Christianity in general. You do not have to defend anyone or anything. History is what it is. The Church is what it is. You do, however, always have to remember that it is the Holy Spirit who is sending you to share your testimony of how faith in Jesus changed your life. It is He who has given you the desire to share God's message of love and forgiveness.

The truth of the matter is that if you were not "converted" or "saved" or "born again" you would not be a "Christian" and most likely not even be reading this. Where would you be, and what would you be doing, if you had not become a disciple of the Lord Jesus? Would you even be alive today? You would probably not be interested in Jesus, Jews, or the eradication of anti-Semitism. It is precisely because your faith was supernaturally imparted to you that you want to be involved in any of this.

It is precisely and exactly because you are a "Christian" that you have a love for the Jewish people and a desire to testify to them about what Jesus has done in your life. This is a foundational truth for you to remember if you are rebuffed for trying to share the Gospel with the Jewish people.

He who began a "good work" in you (Philippians 1:6) is the only one who can begin a "good work" in them. So, relax, let "God Be God" and do His job His way. **As you do this, you will never have a problem keeping your heart and motives pure. You will always be able to remain in the love of God for yourself, for the Jewish people, and for all other people you meet.**

At no time and under no circumstances are you to compromise your faith or testimony. There will be times when you must be *"bold as a lion"* when confronting difficult issues (Proverbs 28:1). You must never hide or, God forbid, be ashamed of your faith in the Lord Jesus (Romans 1:16). You must be willing to risk rejection for your testimony. Don't take it personally. Rejoice in it, and remember that those who reject you today may receive you tomorrow. They may not tell you this, but they will secretly respect you for your conviction and faith. You are, however, to be *"wise as serpents and harmless as doves"* (Matthew 10:16), concerning when and how you share your faith. A simple rule of thumb is this: **Do not answer questions that are not being asked.**

CHAPTER 7 – SHARING YOUR FAITH WITH THE JEWISH PEOPLE

As you walk in love with the Jewish people, God will give you opportunities to *"give the reason for the hope that is within you"* (1 Peter 3:15). But you must wait, as Peter advises, for the questions to be asked. When that happens, you can share your testimony, or Messianic prophecies, or whatever the Lord leads you to do or say. He might give you supernatural *"words of wisdom or knowledge,"* or a *"gift of faith,"* to *"perform miracles"* or *"supernatural healings"* (1 Corinthians 12:8-10). Be open to the direction of the Holy Spirit. The Bible teaches us that the Jews *"require a sign"* (1 Corinthians 1:22), and miracles are hard to argue with!

I pray regularly for a fresh outpouring of miracle-working power upon the Body of Christ, especially as a witness to the Jewish people. You can argue theology and Scripture interpretation, but you cannot argue with a miracle. You can deny it, reject it, ignore it, or try to rationalize it away, but you cannot argue with it. Remember the story of the healing of the young man who was blind from birth. When he was brought before the Synagogue leaders, all he could say in response to their interrogation was, *"Once I was blind, but now I can see"* (John 9:25). They could argue about who Jesus was, but they could not argue with those beautiful, seeing eyes!

If you get confused about the connection between unconditional love (i.e. love without an agenda) and your witness for Jesus, your relationship with the Jewish people will be troubled. Salvation, conversion, redemption, or whatever term you want to use, is an entirely supernatural experience solely dependent upon the will of the Sovereign God. He and He alone determines when and to whom the *"Spirit of Revelation"* comes (John 6:44, 65). We love, bear witness to our faith as we can, and trust God to reveal that Jesus is the Messiah as He will. This is an extremely important point, and it must not be misunderstood or understated.

A significant part of our witness is that our acts of love would provoke questions of interest. I believe that your demonstration of love and support will provoke Jewish people to ask you questions like, "Why are you doing this?" "What is so different about you?" It is the restoration of these dialogues and communication between the Body of Christ and the Jewish people that is central to the eradication of the effects of anti-Semitism.

Instead of people being alienated from one another and having distorted and prejudiced views about each other, we should ask the Lord for ways to open lines of communication with the Jewish people. It is the restoration of these dialogues that will bring opportunities for a new understanding about each other and fresh occasions to share who Jesus is and what He has done in your life. Without the restoration of communication, there will never be those God-appointed opportunities.

As disciples of the Messiah, we do have a mandate to share the good news of the Kingdom of God. However, because the long and painful history of "Christian anti-Semitism" has so damaged the Jewish psyche, evangelism must be done in an extremely sensitive manner. Christians with a heart for the Jewish people will be led by the Lord in different ways of healing those hurts, as well as different ways of being a witness for the Messiah. One thing is certain; as we express the healing Love of God to the Jewish people, we will be witnesses for the *"Prince of Peace"* (Isaiah 9:6) who is the only source of healing (Isaiah 53:5; 1 Peter 2:24).

CHAPTER 8 – HOW DO I GET STARTED?

Practical Guidelines and Suggestions

The first most practical thing you can do is remember that standing against the spirit of anti-Semitism is a supernatural work. If the Lord is calling you into this battle, He will give you great joy and freedom as you cooperate with the Holy Spirit. He will show you that He is leading you by the divine appointments you have, the doors that open, the people you meet, the material that comes your way, and by a myriad of other experiences you will have, both supernatural and natural, that will confirm to you that He is leading you.

I envision the Lord using small groups around the world confronting anti-Semitism and standing with the Jewish people. I see the Holy Spirit giving unique strategies to follow as He makes each group an outpost stationed on the battlefield. These groups can become places where individuals can find like-minded people with whom they can pray, fellowship, learn, and work together. These groups can become havens in the conflict, as we give each other the love and support we need to keep fighting in this spiritual war.

If the Lord leads you to contact your local Synagogue or Temple and speak to the Rabbi or community leader, tell them that you are a Christian seeking to learn more about the "Jewish Roots" of your faith. Tell them that you are renouncing the historical sins of anti-Semitism committed by the Christian Church and that you are seeking ways of reconciliation. Tell them that you want to support the Jewish people and ask them for suggestions about how you can do that in practical ways. Ask them if you can be a part of any activities in the Synagogue. Tell them that you do not have an agenda to evangelize, but to simply build relationships. Tell them that you are not ashamed of your faith, that you believe that Jesus is the Jewish Messiah, and that you will answer questions when asked, but that you are not coming to preach, but to help build relationships between two faith communities that have been estranged for much too long. Tell them that you have a mandate to seek such reconciliation, to stand with the Jewish people against anti-Semitism, and to stand with the nation of Israel. Ask them for their suggestions of practical ways to do this.

There are so many ways you can get involved. Ask the Rabbi if there are classes you can take that will teach you about Jewish history, religion, or the Hebrew language. Ask what books or materials he recommends. If attending classes is not possible, there are many courses online.

Ask the Rabbi about planting a tree in Israel or buying an Israeli bond, or which Jewish organizations they recommend you support or join. Ask the Rabbi to speak at your Church or your home group. A good first subject to ask the Rabbi to speak on would be, "What you want Christians to know about Judaism and the Jewish people." Find out what events the Jewish community is sponsoring and get involved. Go to their annual Holocaust memorial service, or Israel Independence Day celebration. Host a gathering to honor the Church's debt to the Jewish people, or to celebrate Israel. Ask the Jewish community to participate in it. These are just some suggestions. Follow the leading of the Holy Spirit.

As you begin to relate to the Jewish community, be prepared for the possibility that you might be treated with mistrust, suspicion, and skepticism. This is the result of so many centuries of persecution. It is not personal, so don't take it personally. With some rare exceptions, Christians have not historically sought the Jewish people for learning or friendship. Building trust takes time. Be patient and prayerful. God will create and develop the relationships He chooses. Watch Him work! We are living in the days of restoration and reconciliation. You are part of a genuine supernatural work of the Holy Spirit around the world. Watch what the Holy Spirit will do as you give yourself to work with Him in this ministry. If there are no local Synagogues or Temples in your area, ask the Lord to lead you to one that you can begin a correspondence with. Pray about meeting Jewish people in your area that you can build a relationship with. Don't try to do this in the flesh; let the Holy Spirit lead you and guide you. He can arrange some remarkable "divine appointments." Remember, this is a supernatural ministry. When God is leading you, there will be amazing fruit.

CHAPTER 8 – HOW DO I GET STARTED?

Have you ever noticed how, when you're thinking about something you tend to find it, or things about it, in your life? For example, if I ask you think about "red-headed children," you will be amazed at how many of them you begin to notice. The reason for that is that you are making yourself more aware of that particular aspect of your surroundings. As you think and pray about Jewish people and how you can relate to them, you will find yourself being more aware of the Jewish people and Jewish "things" (books, CDs, organizations, artwork, websites, ministries, etc.) that begin to 'appear' in your life. This happens in even greater ways when you pray and ask the Holy Spirit to lead you to the Jewish people and Jewish things that He desires you to find.

You can begin to read and study on your own or in a study group. You may meet people who want to get together to study, but who do not want to do any more than that. That's fine. Drink from as many streams as you can, fellowship with as many different people and groups as you like. Keep your heart open to whomever the Lord leads you to. Learn Jewish history (you will find things you won't find in many Church history books), philosophy, theology, and read about Jewish interpretations of the Bible. You will find much you agree with, and much you don't. Read Jewish translations of the Old Testament and compare them with your English translations. There is wisdom to receive from traditional Jewish sources that have been unknown to most members of the Body of Christ. Be careful as you read. Just because a "Jewish Rabbi" (or a "Christian Minister" – or anyone else for that matter) teaches something, it does not make it true or right. Do not be naïve as you study, but be a wise disciple and follow the admonition written in 1 Thessalonians 5:21, *"Test all things, hold fast to that which is good."* The "things" that are good are those that cause you to mature as a fruitful disciple of the Kingdom of God.

Pray about how you can stand with the Jewish people against their enemies. Here are some things the Lord might lead you to do. Write to Jewish publications or websites declaring your solidarity with the Jewish people and the nation of Israel. Write or email the Israeli embassy in Washington D.C. or one of their local consulates. Do the same to the embassies and consulates of those nations that are not standing with Israel, and to those who are overtly Israel's enemies.

Write to the Secretary General of the UN. Write to your local newspaper and Jewish and Islamic publications. Post things online or create a blog that declares your support. Get involved in organizations and ministries that are already doing such things. Link up with ministries that are helping Jewish people emigrate to the land of Israel. Support ministries that are helping new immigrants with practical aid as they acclimate to living in Israel. Take a trip to Israel and visit the Messianic congregations there. Build personal relationships with the Jewish believers living and ministering in the land and support them in prayer and financially.

If there are Messianic Congregations in your area, build relationships with them as well. Remember, just because they are Messianic, it doesn't mean all of their theology and doctrines are sound. *"Test everything, hold fast to that which is good"* (1 Thessalonians 5:20).

Ask the Lord how you can stand against the spirit of anti-Semitism in the Church. Let Him begin to show you what you can do in your local church or the local churches in your area. Do not despise the day of small beginnings and proceed with wisdom and love. No one is going to receive what they perceive as the "ranting" of a fanatic zealot. Zeal without knowledge and wisdom will do more harm than good. God will show you how to bring this message to the Body of Christ in your community. Be satisfied with small steps and small victories. Wars are won battle by battle, not all at once. Remember the admonition to be *"wise as serpents and gentle as doves"* (Matthew 10:16). You will be amazed what the Lord can do when you have a humble attitude and confidence in the ability of the Holy Spirit to bring truth to His people. Let the Holy Spirit lead you regarding how, and with whom, to share.

Give teaching material to believers you know so they can pass them onto others, including their pastors and elders. You don't have to contact people in authority as much as you do those who have influence. They will use that influence to affect people who have authority. God will open the doors and the hearts of those He is speaking to. Do not allow the enemy to frustrate you or discourage you. Many centuries of anti-Semitic prejudices, theologies, and belief systems are not going to be eradicated overnight. This is a long, intense battle, so relax, enjoy the ride, and leave the 'driving' to the Lord!

CHAPTER 8 – HOW DO I GET STARTED?

As you grow in your understanding of the damage done to the Jewish people by "Christian anti-Semitism," I believe your intercession will deepen for a more powerful demonstration and manifestation of the supernatural love and power of the Holy Spirit in the Body of Christ. **I am convinced that without that supernatural impartation of God's Love and Power, there will not be any meaningful or significant change in the relationship between the Body of Christ and the Jewish people.**

Expressions of support for the Jewish people and the nation of Israel are all well and good, but we must not have an underlying philosophy of "political correctness." We also must never be ashamed of *"the offense of the cross"* (Galatians 5:11) and its testimony of Jesus as Messiah and Lord. Political correctness will never penetrate the hearts of the Jewish people and provoke them to jealousy. They can easily dismiss those well-meaning overtures with an attitude of, "it's about time Christians are finally doing the right thing." That mentality will ultimately put anything to do with Jesus in a place where it can be disregarded as being "for the Gentiles."

My hope and prayer is that those acts of love and kindness will be coupled with supernatural signs and wonders that demonstrate the ultimate reality of the resurrected King of the Jews. May the Jewish people who encounter Him repent and receive Him as their Messiah, Savior, and Lord. May they also go on to be fruitful disciples of the Kingdom of God!

In order to cooperate with the Lord in this ministry, we must continually put ourselves into a spiritual position where the Holy Spirit is free to influence us without hindrance. We must give ourselves the freedom to learn and grow in Him. We must give ourselves and everyone else around us permission to make mistakes. It is through the process of "falling forward" (Proverbs 24:16) that we learn how to cooperate with the Holy Spirit. We see clear evidence of this in the Gospels, as we observe how Jesus used the many failures and mistakes of the disciples as a vehicle for training them.

Because I so highly value your freedom to walk in the Spirit and the freedom we want the Holy Spirit to have as He works with us, I do not have a "formula" to follow or a restrictive list of "do's and don'ts" to obey. Of course, we must recognize that certain words carry emotionally laden baggage for most Jewish people. Because of this, we try to communicate in a way that reflects our understanding of Jewish history and theology. For example, use the word Yeshua instead of Jesus, Messiah instead of Christ, Congregation instead of Church, and New Covenant instead of New Testament. We encourage you to use good old-fashioned common sense as you seek to learn the lessons of history. Pray for revelation as you read from various sources and search the Scriptures. Most of all, listen to the Lord as He speaks to you and directs your steps.

Pray and listen to the strategies of the Holy Spirit as He speaks to you about how to reach out to, and on behalf of, the Jewish people locally, nationally and internationally. Listen to what He tells you to do and how He tells you to do it. Ask the Lord for others to help you. Of course, when it comes to receiving counsel, you have to weigh what you hear from people with what you read in the Scriptures and what you hear in your spirit. The true test of the source of the counsel is the fruit it bears (Matthew 7:17-19). The Word of God will always bear the fruit of the Kingdom of God: righteousness, love, peace, joy and the presence and power of God (Romans 14:17; 1 Corinthians 4:20; Galatians 5:22; Ephesians 5:9).

I invite you to give copies of this book to others who are interested. Open your home and invite people to come and pray and learn. Study our materials and the materials of other ministries. Read, think, listen, discuss, question, pray, and grow! The Holy Spirit will give new revelations, insights, and strategies on how to fight the spirit of anti-Semitism, and we will be able to learn much from others. We must be flexible in responding to the tactics and strategies that God will use as the ebb and flow of the battle changes. We must be *"like the wind"* as the Spirit of God blows upon us in this spiritual fight (John 3:8).

May you obey the last recorded words in the New Testament of perhaps the greatest "Jewish mother" in history, Miriam the mother of Yeshua: *"**Whatever He says to you, DO IT!**"* (John 2:5).

CONTACT INFORMATION

Howard Morgan Ministries
www.HMMin.com
DrM@HMMin.com

In the US
PO Box 956486
Duluth, Ga 30096
770-734-0044
info@HMMin.com

In the UK
0151-652-9956
Karen@HMMin.com

In Canada
250-816-0543
Corrina@HMMin.com